Great Group Leaders

60 Activities to Ignite Identity, Voice, Power, & Purpose

SUSAN RAGSDALE

WC

powerful publications • energetic trainings

write creations group

NASHVILLE, TN

Published by Write Creations Group, LLC, Nashville, TN

www.writecreationsgroup.com

Library of Congress Control Number: 2020918288

ISBN: 978-1-942743-05-7

Editor: Crys Zinkiewicz
Cover Design: Jeenee Lee
Interior Design: Danielle Smith-Boldt
Icons Design: Linda Ragsdale

To Justin Crowe, a dear friend, inspiration, and self-identified #1 fan!
"It's for the children!"

"Ignite" is the essence of *Great Group Leaders*...Susan Ragsdale takes you beyond the principles of Stephen Covey's best-selling *Seven Habits of Highly Effective People*. She provides unique leadership tools for individual, organizational, and community change.

    —**Patty Watson,** Nonprofit Leadership Consultant

One of the abilities that God has given humans is the capacity for self-awareness. Knowing our own self is a gift. And self-deception is a sure path to a meaningless life. Susan Ragsdale offers us a guided expedition into the wilderness of who we are. Walk with her there. You may discover you.

    —**Dan Boone,** President, Trevecca Nazarene University; author of *A Charitable Discourse: Talking About the Things That Divide Us*

Many books on leadership provide readers with general ideas that are difficult to put into practice in the real world. In contrast, in *Great Group Leaders* Susan Ragsdale gives us practical activities that make it easy to lead in ways that are collaborative, empowering, wonderfully uplifting.

    —**Kent Pekel,** President and CEO of Search Institute

The activities in *Great Group Leaders* have at their core the emotional intelligence essentials of knowing yourself and leading others. The increasing levels of vulnerability and connection make this a powerful tool to shape the leaders of tomorrow. Susan Ragsdale has written a treasure of a book that is packed with fun, encouragement, and challenge.

    —**Nancy Reece,** Participating Faculty, Leadership & Coaching (Retired), Lipscomb University, Pfeffer Graduate School of Business; co-author of *Strengthening the Organizational Heart;* author of *The Dichotomy of Power*

This book is an amazing resource for leaders of all types of groups/organizations. The exercises are incredibly well thought out, explained and allow for deeper exploration and discussion. Susan Ragsdale has once again proven her ability to provide opportunities for deeper connections with people of all ages.

    —**Tara Brown,** the Connection Coach & Speaker; author of *Different Cultures/Common Ground*

MAIN MENU

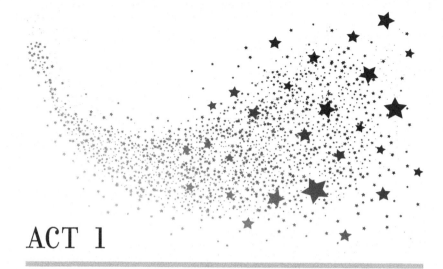

ACT 1

Making This Book Work for You

It takes courage to grow up and become who you really are.

—E.E. CUMMINGS

Man did not weave the web of life,
he is merely a strand in it.
Whatever he does to the web,
he does to himself.

—NATIVE AMERICAN PROVERB

You cannot teach a man anything,
you can only help him discover it in himself.

—GALILEO GALILIEI

Full Speed Ahead

The underlying premise for the activities in this book is that each of us—young and old—has power within ourselves, through our words, actions, and example, to exert influence for the common good. We lead from within. We have power, voice, and purpose that are ours to tap and share. It is up to us to use that power. But how do we discover our purpose? How do we know what means something to us? What abilities do we have to offer? That's part of the journey of exploration. Those are just a few of the questions we all encounter time and time again.

This book, then, with its guided activities is about and for everyone. While not a how-to book and no promises for how to become the leader we always imagined in seven easy steps, it will take us on an adventure that can shape our lives. Which is a good thing because learning to hone our leadership capacity is a lifelong endeavor. The activities here just make it more fun for young and old alike.

This book offers an invitation to join the journey of self-discovery to find our own unique purpose within the world, learn to own our lives, and offer the same regard, acceptance, and respect to others. Then, together, we can begin to become world changers within our chosen spheres of influence. This journey, while very individual, is done within the context of a shared group experience.

Discovering and developing our own power isn't easy. Every day conflicting demands, opinions, and competing values vie for our attention. To sort through all the clamor to clearly hear our own inner whisperings of wisdom is a challenging task. However, once we learn to recognize our own voice, become comfortable with ourselves, and can name what is most important to us, THEN we can live and lead our lives from a centered place of selfhood. We can lead from within.

This discovery is true for us and for the individuals in our group. Let's open the door for everyone to access their gifts and discover their inner purpose. Let's help the individuals in our group realize their own inner beauty as well as show them the possibilities of what they can achieve when they tap, claim, and use their own power.

Within These Pages

The activities throughout these pages are geared to help each person discover their inner brilliance within the leadership movements of self and leading with others. These undertakings are the overarching themes:

- In the **Discover & Stretch** section, individuals will self-identify traits and passions they wish to possess, delve into values and people who influence them, and explore their own sense of purpose and power as leaders.

- In the **Leading With Others** activities, participants learn to navigate respect for others and stretch to see others' experiences as equal to their own. They will realize the importance of embracing awareness, reflection, and empathy.

Each activity is written in a recipe style format. For each process, you will see—

ACTIVITY TITLE

Time—indicates the amount of time it takes to complete the activity from start to debrief (based on a group size of 6–15 people)

Supplies—points to any materials you will need to gather that are germane to the success of the process (note: you will probably have most items on hand)

Prep—specifies any tasks best done before group time

DIRECTIONS Directions—gives the step-by-step instructions for leading the activity

Going Deeper—models possible conversation starters you can use after completing the activity to build upon what happened and deepen the experience

The sequence of query in the **Going Deeper** section builds and expands outward. For example, the first prompts let the group talk about the activity. Next, the group talks about what they are learning individually. Lastly, the conversation broadens to reflect on ideas and views about the group or the community as a whole. The inquiry deliberately ties the event back to life, emphasizing relevance and enhancing critical thinking skills.

> The **Going Deeper** segments provided are by no means limiting. The questions are a tool that may save you some work. The prompts are there to model how to guide the dialogue from the activity itself to more meaningful, in-depth connections. With that in mind, you are free to adapt what is here—including adjusting the time to allow more for larger groups and reflective teams or to simply build in extra minutes so as not to rush through the conversation, especially if something vital pops up. You can also change the questions altogether. Ask whatever naturally evolves from what's happening in your group. In fact, I encourage you to pay attention to them! Do, however, take advantage of the moment to *maximize learning and growth.* Don't stop with simply debriefing the mechanics of the activity (i.e., What was difficult about this game? What was easy?) Push for meaning. Challenge participants to reflect, think, learn and grow—from self and each other.

Leadership Myths and Truths

Myth Busters

Ask any five people how they define leadership and what comes to mind, and two answers arise: "I'm not a leader" and "Leadership is a formal position. It's one person in charge who tells others what to do. It happens from a top-down approach." The problem with these two thoughts is that people will dismiss the idea of themselves as leaders, thus stunting their own potential from the onset as well as being blind to the many ways in which people lead.

However, as you continue the given conversation and ask about leadership qualities, people answer with traits such as "vision, empathy, serving others, creativity, innovation, improvement (of self or situations), management skills, and the ability to make a difference." Ah! Something deeper is at work. People know what great leadership looks like. They do. They can name the qualities and they know good leadership in action when they see it. They simply struggle with leading or influencing others to lead in the way they want. So, when your group starts naming the traits that were named above, call a timeout to point out what was just said. Did the speakers hear what they just said?

"Wait a minute. Do you consider yourself empathetic? Do you serve in some way? Do you manage your schoolwork, schedule, or family time? Is there something you're trying to improve in your life?" Yes. "Then perhaps we need to rethink how we define leadership and what it actually is."

To that end, let's address two leadership myths and put them to rest—

Myth #1: **There are natural born leaders and then there are the rest of us.** Not true. It is easy to look at well-known leaders over time, such as Saint Theresa of Calcutta or Martin Luther King, Jr., and hold them apart as holy, special, touched from birth (or whatever qualifier you want to assign them). That distance we put in place creates a separation that says they had that something extra that we don't have. We can never be a Saint Theresa or do what she did. We can never achieve what Dr. King has achieved. This myth just excuses us from ever using the power, capacities, and assets we do have. We never even try. Why bother?

This same separation thinking is visible in professional sports. Pick any of the sports stars. They are frequently singled out and held in awe. And yet, pros get as good as they do because of the hundreds or thousands of hours of practice that help them perfect their techniques. They put in the work to get the results they want to see. They fall down, they fail, and they learn—time and again—to keep getting back up. They get back up more often than they stay down. The choice to try again makes the difference.

We have potential within us. We have gifts waiting to be realized. *Our* gifts. But somehow, we judge them as not good enough when we think in terms of leadership. But those skills are there, within us, waiting to be tapped, waiting to be expressed in actions, small and large.

Myth #2: **Leadership is formal; it's a position for those in charge.** People's thoughts commonly turn to positions of authority, either elected officials or head honchos of companies upon hearing the descriptor "leader." You've probably even seen in one or more sci-fi movies, an alien descending from its ship saying, "Take me to your leader." One version even said take me to your President. This snapshot illustrates our second clash of myth versus fact.

Formal leadership is only one *type* of leadership. Knowing who's in charge in any given club, organization, or political structure easily identifies this type. You can point to a chart or list of titles and know who's who. The primary association of the word *leader* to formal or political positions as THE platform for expressing voice and power leaves leadership as exclusive and inaccessible. Leadership, from this viewpoint, becomes restricted to a small number of people. The fact is these positions are just that—*positions,* roles in a job that require someone to manage specified duties and people. The positions don't actually say anything about what kind of leader is filling the role.

The truth is we have opportunities to lead every day by our choices, words, and actions. We can lead by the quality of how we live out our lives.

A New Leadership Order

This reframing of our understanding of leadership is essential in order for us to evolve and maximize our own potential. First, we must know what we truly believe when it comes to leadership. (Dispel those myths!) Why? Because we pass on what we know. So, if we want our group of young people (or peers) to realize their full human potential, then we need to be ready to address our own myths and misgivings and grapple with our own understanding. Second, we must debunk the idea of leadership of the few and embrace the idea of leadership being an "all-play."

While the definitions for leadership are many, the one that resonates most with my belief in everyone's inner capacity to lead is one I first learned in a workshop series from Search Institute out of Minneapolis:

Leadership is exerting influence for the common good.

I offer that definition here to build on our new grasp of leadership and to give readers a frame of reference to embrace. Consider leadership, as well, in light of these quotes—

Your work is to discover your work and then, with all your heart, to give yourself to it.

—BUDDHA

If your actions inspire others to dream more, learn more, do more and become more, you are a leader.

—JOHN QUINCY ADAMS

Life is what you make it. Your end, your legacy, is a compilation of the choices you make and the subsequent consequences of those choices. You must lead your movement in life.

—DAN HORGAN, TELL ME I CAN'T AND I WILL

Collectively, these three quotes express an underlying belief that everyone is a leader in their own right. Leadership is about the influence each of us has and how we use it. Being a leader is about who we are—our capacities and choices to exert influence. The only variable is the scale to which we express our inner gifts.

Our essential task then, as guides on this pathway of self-discovery, is to uphold this belief in each person, point out when we see the individuals in our group tapping and using their own power for good, and encourage them to find ways to use their voice, power, and purpose that stem from their sense of identity and their relationship to the world around them.

To help illustrate what I'm talking about, we'll turn to cultural icons of science fiction to help illuminate some key points.

To Go Where No One Has Gone Before

Growing up, I could be found every week in front of the television for one exciting hour. I was watching *Star Trek*. The opening music, the words of the mission, and the vision of the USS *Enterprise* flying through space swept me away. Through the *Enterprise's* weekly explorations, I met new people; I watched as civilizations engaged and found that seemingly elusive common ground for forging new relationships. I saw what happened when they couldn't work through differences. But ever, always, I had hope—hope for a better future where we would work together and expand beyond our own lives to *be* more.

It was *Star Trek* and *Star Wars* that first inspired thinking around the framework for this book. With a prompt from a fellow author and publisher, Nicole Givens Kurtz, my thinking started clicking into place and ideas flowed together as I reflected on lessons learned from sci-fi and how well they exemplified in an instinctual way what I feel when I think about what leadership means to me. The Force is available to all. *Star Wars* teaches us there is a Dark Side, and it must be confronted. Resistance to evil is not futile (*Star Trek: Next Generation* and *Star Wars*).

Yoda warns us of what can happen when we fail to heed our own thoughts, emotions and beliefs, and how quickly actions can lead us astray...toward using the Force for evil intent. We know that darkness inside of ourselves. We know what our shadow side looks like. We know that power used for ill seeks to destroy the "resistance" (in *Star Wars* that refers to those who sought a better life for all) in the form of viewpoints, ways of life, and ideology. We see what absolute obedience to one ruler will cost when diversity of thought, expression, and life are found intolerable.

From *Star Trek*, we learn about possibilities. We see what can be and how we can act upon a core mission that is inclusive, kind, humane, and expansive. The crew of the *Enterprise,* episode after episode, sets out on its mission in space to explore strange new worlds (translation: current contemporary issues), to seek out new life and new civilizations (other cultures and beliefs), and to boldly go where no man (later changed to "no one") has gone before (establishing new laws, culture, and beliefs in the wake of those explorations).

Sometimes, the *Enterprise* runs into civilizations more advanced than humanity. Sometimes, those more advanced declare humanity not ready for higher thinking, processes, or technology. And, in those moments, the crew of the *Enterprise* makes their case for humankind: We have our faults, but we are learning. We learn from our mistakes. We learn from each culture. We strive for something more for the whole universe. Thus, no one should count us out.

In keeping with these thematic life lessons, questions arise: *What does it mean to be human today? Who are we as a people? Who do we want to become in the future as a people, as a society, as a world? What will our future selves look like? What will our world look like?*

The good news is that we create our answers by the choices we make and the actions we take. We shape the future.

Courtesy of *Star Wars* and *Star Trek*, below are four of the many teachings I've gleaned befitting development of self and our life together. These ideas can help us (and I do mean *us*—facilitators and the groups we shepherd) shape our future with intention as we prepare ourselves and our young people to lead in a diverse world from a place of self-understanding, compassion for others, and a commitment to the world they want to create. The lessons are—

1. **The Force exists, welcoming and readily available.** It is with us, within us, and we can tap into it whenever and as often as we want to do good. The Force flows and is a natural, inexhaustible, dynamic energy that renews us. The choice is ours to use power for good.

2. **Understanding is a strength of forward motion.** Yoda warns us that "Fear is the path to the Dark Side. Fear leads to anger. Anger leads to hate. Hate leads to suffering." Empathy is needed. When we set aside that which divides us in favor of seeking out greater truths, pursuits, and endeavors, we evolve. In *Star Wars*, we advance in our Jedi powers. In *Star Trek*, we are able to engage with cultures different from us without loss of our own identity.

3. **Stay true to the mission.** Explore and seek to know and befriend the unknown. The universe is more beautiful than we know, full of interesting places, traditions, notions, philosophies, life—all kinds of life from painted buntings and caracals to fairy circles and the northern lights—and adventures. Diversity flows at all levels of life and has value. Every species, every individual is needed. With each encounter and new experience, we become more.

We're better versions of ourselves—more open, more compassionate, more humane.

4. **Never stop exploring and learning.** Attitude is everything. Being open to other ideas, cultures, communities, and ways of doing things keep us reflective and growing. Staying curious keeps us wide-eyed to the wonder of who we are as individuals and as a human race. The future is "the undiscovered country. People can be very frightened of change," Captain Kirk says, quoting another character in the movie *The Undiscovered Country.* But to change is to evolve. We need to be mindful of becoming closed off to anything out of our comfort zone, and resist immediate dismissal of another just because they or their thoughts and ideas seem alien. With each encounter, we can practice flexibility, empathy, critical thinking, and adaptability as we imagine life in someone else's shoes.

The future is full of possibilities. We help shape that future. Every person, every opportunity, and every experience can broaden our perspective and enlarge our understanding of what it means to be human. Each of these encounters extend our awareness of the vastness and value of all life on this planet earth. We are one of many nestled in a much larger universe.

May the Force be with you as you seek to create change within self, others, and the world. Go boldly. The world needs you. You need you. What will you do?

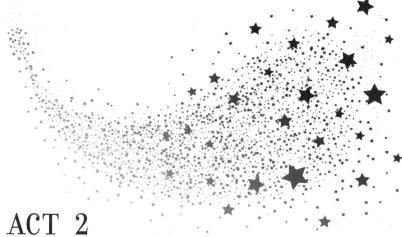

ACT 2

Discover & Stretch

The Force is what gives a Jedi his power. It's an energy field created by all living things. It surrounds us, it penetrates us, it binds the galaxy together.

—OBI-WAN IN EPISODE 4: A NEW HOPE

At the center of your being you have the answer; you know who you are, and you know what you want.

—LAO TZU

The Force Is Strong With This One

I can think of no better illustration that represents leadership as the *power to exert influence* than that found in the *Star Wars* movies. You already know where I'm going with this. The Force.

The Force? Yes, THE Force—that one. If I could evenly, grammatically swap out the word *leader* for *Star Wars'* use of the Force, I would.

In the movies, the Force is portrayed as a vital essence—an energy field—that each of us can harness. The Force connects us to one another and to all of life: people, the earth, trees, animals, plant life, the sun, moon—everything. The internal vitality of the Force is comprised of meaning, purpose, and connection to something bigger than ourselves alone. The Force is accessible within every single person.

Thus, everyone has the capacity to draw on the Force to influence life around us. For good. Or, for ill. It all depends upon our choices. We impact the people and the world around us every day with our intentions, choices, words, and actions. Our choices have consequences. Those results have a ripple effect that, in turn, interacts with others' choices and influences. These intersections may clash or collaborate to become an even more powerful ripple.

The impact depends on how we live and lead. Since this book is dedicated to great group leaders, my hope is that everyone will tune their lives to the Force and use their power to exert their influence for good—the common good, the well-being of all.

Know Your Group

For those of you who aren't *Star Wars* fans, let's visualize what I'm talking about in your program space. Picture your 20 young people. Some of them are self-motivated. Many of them are eager to jump in and get involved with whatever project or cause your group happens to be focused on. All of them are passionate. They're young people! Of course, they're full of passion as well as idealism, energy, and opinions about what's going on in the world. They are biologically gifted at this age to crave novelty and to be risk takers. (You can read a bit more about this natural drive in Ann Saylor's and my book *Groups, Troops, Clubs & Classrooms: The Essential Handbook for Working With Youth.*)

Give young people the opportunity and that fire within them will turn into action when their attention is captured by an event, a cause, or a situation. They are eager to get involved and are adept at mobilizing peers and resources to get things done. That idealism. That energy. That risk taking. That desire to do good. It's there. It's within them. And "no" is not a word that holds them back from trying. These are your Jedis.

Also, within your group are those who have power and have not made the best choices with that power. They lead, but they use their power to cause harm rather than to do good. But that doesn't mean they're lost causes. You see the potential. You just need to redirect their potential and energies toward more positive outlets.

And finally, you will have some who don't see their own potential or recognize that they have power. Life has tripped them up. Or, maybe opportunities simply haven't been provided to them yet to tap into their own power and realize that their gifts make a huge difference in the world.

Regardless of where they are, each one has within them a natural desire to leave a mark on the world. We just need to introduce them to the Force and train them in the ways of self-understanding, compassion, and mastery.

Jedi Training Begins Here

Our journey to learn how to tap the Force and use our power starts with self-understanding. Going inward to explore and get to know the leader within is a necessary part of development. And inward is where each of us returns time and again to self-check, reflect, listen, learn, and evolve. Self-mastery is equally satisfying and hard work.

Satisfying—because we are learning the depth and dimensions of our own inner make-up: *What inspires me? What is my passion? What do I like and enjoy? What am I good at doing? When am I most joyful and what am I doing in that moment?*

Hard work—because when we turn within, we are bombarded by fear, anger, judgments, and insecurities. In learning to master self, we have to face and wrestle with our own particular inner demons. We struggle with and learn to accept our frailties and weaknesses. And then, we face and wrestle with them, again and again, because our thoughts and emotions are always with us clamoring to control us instead of us, them.

It takes patient work to take charge, own our lives, and be our own person, our own leader. Mastering self is no easy task. The commitment to do so is for a lifetime. But the investment to do so has huge payoffs. When we pay attention to our inner wise teacher, we make discoveries. We name and claim our talents, passions, and quirkiness. We grasp that we have everything we need (the Force) to manage our emotions and thought life. And, we find that that seemingly insurmountable task IS possible. Our pursuit has us growing into our abilities to work through struggles, overcome adversity, stand up when we fall down, and share generously from our hearts.

Self-mastery is the work of Jedis. Every Jedi will tell you that to be in concert with the Force is worth all the discipline, focus, and work required. Investing in the treasure you carry within your being that only you can offer everyone around you is valuable. The fulfillment of the purpose that you are uniquely crafted to complete ensures the work is meaningful. The gain of self-knowing, inner peace, and self-compassion is priceless.

These fruits can only be obtained when you quit trying to be everyone else and fully embrace your own unique purpose and destiny. That gift to the world that you carry inside you just by being you manifests when you accept and take responsibility to own your own life and create a life of well-being. The step of self-understanding, then, is the first step of real leadership.

Using Cultural Relevance

You may be nodding in agreement especially about the part where I say that it takes work to know who we really are, become comfortable with our faults and failures, learn, grow, and mature, and to identify our life's purpose. And if it's hard for us, imagine how much harder it is for our young people!

Passing on the importance of knowing self and constantly striving to do and be better to the young people you care about—I can see you laughing while crying at the same time. Yes, we want them to know themselves, grow into their strengths, self-actualize, have a guiding moral compass, recognize their spiritual essence, and so much more.

This is why I am modeling using terms like "the Force" and "boldly go where no one has gone before" to try to impart all we hope for our youth to them. Those images carry oomph and pizzazz. Using cultural relevance, you can hook your group and to communicate a much deeper relevance. Sci-fi is one way. There are others: Harry Potter, anime, The Hunger Games, superheroes (which I also will make use of and have in other books). Adapt and connect with what works for you and your group to engage their curiosity, sense of adventure, and willingness for self-discovery. And, make it fun.

Know Yourself: Warts & All

Answering the question, *Who am I?* is the journey of a lifetime. The activities in the **Discover & Stretch** section provide a means for participants to start with where they are. As their guides, we want to continue to help point the way inward for them to explore a deeper knowing. We also want to create a safe space for them to test their ideas, values, beliefs, and fledgling understanding with the group. We've all said things we don't believe until we say them out loud, hear ourselves, and rethink. In our Yoda assigned roles, we should continue to ask, prompt, and push for self-understanding and discovery while maintaining a brave space for sharing.

Your group will assess their own hearts and thoughts—an important, thoughtful reflective action to take before moving into deliberate action. The activities in this book ask young leaders to think about their understanding of leadership, diversity, and empathy, as well as assumptions they may unintentionally hold. The processes help equip young people to know themselves better, to respect all people, and to set a course for positive change.

Don't Forget:

With group work, you can lead them through processes and activities that stir curiosity, ignite wonder, and prompt them to turn to critical-thinking and reflection. The experiences you create set the stage for exploration. Encourage them. Keep it safe to share. Safeguard each person's vulnerability and authenticity. Reiterate often the importance of having a space where everyone can speak up. Tend the space well. Teach them to truly see and listen to each other.

Prompt bravery to speak truths or to speak up. Gently invite them to get to know and become more comfortable in their own skin.

Ask questions—ones you don't know the answer to and that don't lead them to what you want to hear. Ask queries that call for a thoughtful pause. Encourage silence and reflection. As they take a moment to consider, remind them to ask *themselves* what they think and know. Remember to make the questions for each activity your own. You can use them as is, or as a springboard for other questions you see need to be asked.

You or We?

The *you* in the **Going Deeper** prompts indicate
questions to individuals. The use of the word *we*
indicates a shift in the questions to the group as a
whole, thinking about themselves as a cohesive unit.

Do not be discouraged if it takes the group awhile to evolve.
It may be a slow process for them to begin to articulate what is
meaningful for them about their own lives. Keep asking. Keep
creating the space. Keep showing interest in what they think, know,
and experience.

They will begin to know and understand themselves. You are the
one who is coaching them on this beautiful journey of self-discovery.
This self-awareness of the richness each of us has inside ourselves is
one of the greatest gifts that any of us can offer another.

DISCOVER & STRETCH

Activities

It is easier to destroy than it is to create. The real work of life is to consciously create the life we want to live, and by way of doing so contribute to creating a world we want to live in.

It is easy to tear someone down, discredit the ideas of others, and cast doubt on dreams. It is more difficult to support others and lift them up, enrich the ideas of others and empower people to pursue their dreams.

But harder still to do so for ourselves.

—JESSE KRIEGER, AUTHOR OF LIFESTYLE ENTREPRENEUR,
FOUNDER OF LIFESTYLE ENTREPRENEURS PRESS

I DO TOO!

 5–10 minutes

 statements

DIRECTIONS Gather the group in a seated circle. Read each statement and ask the group to jump up and point both of their thumbs toward their chests saying, "I do too!" if the statement is true for them. Explain that the intent of this exercise is to get a feel for what people think and their experiences in volunteering and leadership thus far.

Explain that the first statement is a practice round. The statement is: *I like pizza.* Restate that anyone who likes pizza should jump up, point their thumbs toward their chest and yell, "I do too!" After a pause, ask those who are standing to sit down.

Do as many statements as desired. Adapt statements as needed for your particular group.

Statements

- I have skills and talents I can put to work to better my community.
- I have been in charge of or want to start a project or initiative to address a community need.
- I believe it's important to be actively involved in volunteering and serving others.
- I know young people can impact issues.
- I want to make the world a better place.
- I have ideas for what we can do to address some community problems.
- I have a cause I care about greatly.
- I see myself as a leader.
- I believe it is important to vote.
- I have participated or currently participate in march-ins or sit-ins or in candlelight ceremonies.
- I have written or currently write to political officials or newspapers to express my opinions on pressing issues.

- I have helped or currently help advocate for peers and others to get involved in community issues.
- I speak up or out for people and issues I care about.
- I believe that what happens in another country or even another town affects me.
- I care about people and what happens to them…even those I don't know personally.
- When I see someone being treated wrongly or unfairly, I believe it's important to take some kind of action.
- I eagerly want to be involved in making a difference.

Going Deeper

- How did it feel to hear other voices saying, "I do too!" in agreement with you?
- What did you learn about yourself from this activity?
- What is one thing you are proud of about yourself?
- Which statements excite you because there were multiple voices in agreement?
- Which statements stood out to you because there weren't that many voices in agreement, but that statement was important to you?
- What other statements would you like declared to see what our group thinks or has experienced with regards to serving and/or leading?
- What is the cause you'd like to hear everyone say, "I do too!" when it comes to solving that need in the world?

FLYING QUESTIONS

 20 minutes

 copy paper
writing utensils

DIRECTIONS, Ask participants to think about a question they would like everyone in the room to answer. It should be something they are curious about or something that is really important to them. (*ex: What book is your favorite? What is something you do that brings you great joy?*)

Give everyone an 8½ by 11 sheet of paper and have them write their questions on the paper, and then fold the paper into paper airplanes. Allow 2 minutes to complete the task.

Gather the group in a circle. On a signal, everyone flies their planes into the middle of the circle. All participants pick up a new airplane and unfold them to determine the question they will answer aloud.

Take turns having volunteers read aloud their question, then answering them. If time allows, you can have more than the volunteer answer any given question.

Variation #1:

Give each participant a balloon to blow up and tie off as they think, and then have them write their question(s) on their balloon.

On "go," everyone tosses the balloons in the air and bats them about until you say stop. When you say stop, everyone should grab a balloon. If someone gets their original question, they should swap balloons with another person.

Variation #2:

Have a participant read the question on their balloon and tap it to someone else in the circle to answer. After answering, that person taps the balloon they were holding to someone else. Continue tapping and answering questions until everyone has had a turn.

Game in Action

Here are some sample questions that surfaced when played this game as a "get to know you" bonding activity with adult students in the Humphrey's International Fellowship Program at Vanderbilt University. These professionals had come from around the world to the U.S. for a one-year youth educational program.

- What do you like?
- Are you a good cook? What's your favorite thing to cook?
- What do you do when you are blue?
- Tell us about a funny moment in your life.
- What is your greatest ambition?
- What is your favorite movie?
- What is the best memory from your childhood?
- What do you believe about God?

Going Deeper

- What did you learn from this activity?
- How does sharing things we are interested in or want to learn about help us connect with others?
- What follow up questions do you want to ask someone to learn more about what they said?
- Why is asking questions important to growing as a person?
- What are other things you are curious about and want to know?

A-Z SKILLS

 8–15 minutes

 none

DIRECTIONS Divide the group into teams. Explain that you will call out a letter of the alphabet. For each letter called, team members should think of a realistic or unique way they can contribute to the group that starts with that letter, either a skill they bring to the group or something they can lead or teach, probably something that no one else in the group knows or can do.

Once someone on a team thinks of something, the person from that team speed walks to the facilitator, tags them and shares out loud for the whole group a way they contribute to the team. For example, if the facilitator calls out the letter H, someone might say "I can teach proper use of hash tags" or "I can share 2 tips on healthy eating habits."

Go over the rules. One point is awarded to the team that shares a true contribution first. If others on the opposite team doubt the contribution or simply are curious and want to know more, they can challenge the statement shared. The player must then "prove" abilities or knowledge in some way. Only 4 challenges allowed per team.

Variations

If the group knows one another well, vary this activity by having the group build up others in the group. After a letter is called, when someone tags the facilitator, they must name someone else from their team and what they do well that starts with the letter. Or, the entire group must agree on one thing they all can do starting with a given letter.

DOWN THE LINE

 15–20 minutes

 questions list

DIRECTIONS Divide the group into two teams. Have them stand in straight lines that face each other. Each person should be standing directly across from a partner. Give pairs 35 seconds each to answer a question given.

Announce time after 35 seconds to indicate when the other partner should talk. Once both members of the pair are done sharing, have one group line rotate one person down the line (dancing down the middle of the entire group is encouraged and allowed to add energy!) while the other group line stays in place.

Everyone now has a new partner. Give a new question and repeat the timing process. Use as many questions as desired. Choose the category of questions that fit your focus.

Once done, gather the group in a circle. Ask for a few volunteers to share what stood out the most from their conversations. What did they learn about themselves? What did they discover was really important to them?

Leadership Questions

- What do you love to learn about?
- What inspires you?
- What motivates you and gives you energy to press on despite any opposition?
- What have you learned about perseverance?
- What have you learned about making big decisions?
- How are you a positive influence on your friends and family?
- How do you actively practice setting and keeping healthy boundaries?
- Describe a time when it was difficult to tell the truth, but you did anyways. What happened?
- What is the most important quality a leader can have that you highly value?

- What have you learned about respect from people who are different from you?
- What (particular skill) artistic ability do you have or wish you could further develop?
- What is your leadership style? How does your influence show up in what you do?
- Describe a time when you helped someone else out.
- What gives your life a sense of meaning and purpose?
- What are you most proud of about yourself?

 Facilitator's Note

One way to use this activity with new groups especially is to start with easy, get-to-know-you inquiries and progress into the more in-depth ones. Be sure to pick out the questions ahead of time depending on your group make up. Depending on the group, a skilled facilitator may vary the time as people become more comfortable and questions are more in depth. For example, you may want to vary by 15 seconds at a time, adding 15 seconds to deeper questions if you want them to have more time to reflect and answer. You also may have groups that finish talking more quickly. That's why it's important to keep an eye on the group rather than the timer. Make sure you monitor what is happening in the group and adjust accordingly.

Character Questions

- When you were a child, who was someone you considered a good role model? Why?
- Describe a time when you felt you were being treated unfairly. What happened and how did you respond?
- Who taught you the most about the importance of being trustworthy? How did they teach you?
- What value do you hold in high regard?

- Which value is easier for you to live: caring for others or being responsible? Why?
- Which value is easier for you to live out: being selfless, or having a high integrity? Why?
- What character values do you most want to model for your friends, family, and community? Why?
- Which value is more challenging for you to live out: promoting equality or exhibiting restraint? Why?
- Which value is more challenging for you to live out: speaking a truth despite possible negative reactions or standing up for someone who can't stand up for themselves?
- Who is someone you respect for his or her character? Why?
- What sends a message of care to you?
- How do you show you are a responsible person? At home? In the community? At work?

STRENGTHS WALK

 10–15 minutes

 list of strengths

DIRECTIONS, Explain that you are going to call out a strength and that you want participants to arrange themselves on a continuum depending on how much of a strength the called one is for them personally. They will walk to the place that best fits their opinion.

Designate one side of the room as "strong," the middle as "some or a little" and the other end of the room as "not so much." For each strength named, ask 1–2 people to share examples of how they use that strength in their life.

Strengths

- time management
- planning
- conflict resolution
- motivation
- encouragement
- organization
- communication skills
- artistic
- public speaking
- teaching
- discernment

- marketing
- budgeting
- vision
- guidance
- transparency
- authenticity
- resilience
- courage
- nurturing
- integrity

Variation

Use this activity as an affirmation for groups that know one another well. When strengths are called out, ask the group, "Who do you think displays this strength really well?" Or call on Melanie, for example, to name five people in the group she thinks possess these particular strengths.

Going Deeper

- Which of the strengths called do you feel is a primary strength for you in your life?
- What other strengths do you have that weren't mentioned?
- Which strengths do you use the most frequently?
- When you think of a leader, which type of strength do you think is more important for you to use: being end results oriented or being people focused? Why?
- Is it easy to balance getting things done and paying attention to others when it comes to leading others? Why or why not?
- What strengths do you need or want to further develop for yourself? What are some ideas you have for doing this?

IDENTITY

 10–15 minutes

 slips of paper
writing utensils

DIRECTIONS Ask the group to define the word "identity." Let them discuss the various meanings and interpretations they have. Explain that identity includes many aspects of what makes each of us who we are: *traditions, individual characteristics, beliefs, values, and the groups we belong to and gravitate toward.* Some of our identity is fixed (eye color and skin color) and some of it we create for ourselves (becoming a musician, joining a robotics team).

Distribute paper and writing utensils to everyone. Ask them to write down their name and three facts about their identity. Two facts can be anything at all. But, one fact should be the most interesting, unique, or most likely not to be known by others in the group. For example, my great-great-grandmother was full-blooded Cherokee Indian. Or, our family tradition includes giving family members three presents: one educational, one fun, and one to share with another. Or my basketball team's mantra is "You do the best you can with the strength and energy you have each day."

Give them 2–3 minutes to work.

When time is up, collect the papers. Redistribute and have each person read aloud what was written. The rest of the group tries to guess who the card is describing.

Going Deeper

- Was it difficult or easy to identify others from what was written?
- What fact surprised you about someone? Why?
- What did you notice about the choices that were made for identity? Did we pick similar things or very different aspects?
- What did you notice that others thought was important about identity? Did similar things get mentioned or did we highlight different aspects?

- What identity do we want to create as a group? What traits do we want to be known for? When we serve or work in the community, what do we want others to see that we value?
- How will we interact within our group and how will we engage with the bigger world, however we define that world? How will we create a space of belonging, respect, and acceptance of others?

KEY INFLUENCERS

 15–20 minutes

 paper
writing utensils
selected issue perspectives

 Create a list of issue perspectives you want the group to weigh in on or choose from this list: *climate change, safety in schools, immigration, free higher education, poverty, discrimination, gun control, minimum wage*

DIRECTIONS Ask everyone to draw a smiley face in the middle of their paper and label it with their name. Next, invite them to draw 4–5 circles surrounding their faces. Invite them to think about their whole day and where they spend most of their time: home, school, neighborhood, community gathering places, with friends, places of faith—synagogues, churches or mosques—or on social media and devices. Ask them to identify from all of these choices, who the key people and places are that influence their thinking, beliefs, and values the most; whom they respect; whom they listen to; and who influences their opinions and thinking.

Give them 2–3 minutes to jot down or doodle images inside each of the 4–5 circles to represent the Key Influencers.

Next, explain that you will call out an issue and will ask for a volunteer to state what their view is about the given matter and name the person(s) who has had the most influence on their way of thinking. After the opinion is given, ask if there is a different perspective on that subject that someone else has (and where that influence came from). Remind the group that this activity is about identifying Key Influencers, it is not a time to debate anyone's views.

Call out an issue perspective and solicit responses. Then, have the group gather into teams of 3–4 to discuss their Key Influencers and how they have shaped their outlooks and ideas. What do they tribute to each of these influences? Give them 5 minutes to chat.

Wrap up with a few points such as: It's important to recognize that how we view the world is swayed both by those around us and our actual experiences. The experiences and people who have been part of our Key Influencers' lives have also shaped them. And so, it continues backward and forward as we will shape others' lives. We need to be appreciative of the contributions of those who have shaped us while also learning to apply our own critical thinking and understanding to current community issues and decisions.

We do this to ensure we make the best decisions possible in any given situation. It's also important to surround ourselves with positive influencers who seek to bring out the best in us and acknowledge our gifts, talents, and contributions.

Step In, Step Out

We can *step in* to lead in the moment—a speaker doesn't show up and we give the talk; someone falls and needs help getting up; we see someone being treated unfairly and advocate or help them. We can *step out* to be front and center leading the pack—like the students from the Parkland High School shooting who register people to vote and are working on law changes. Young people during the COVID-19 pandemic showed how powerful they are. Stories abound of clubs and individuals who have made masks, distributed sanitation items to homeless people, redistributed food, run errands, set up online homework assistance, organized free babysitting, and disseminated public health information in their own local communities.

Going Deeper

- Who are some of the Key Influencers you identified?
- How have they shaped what you think, value, and believe?
- What do you value about what you have gained from their insights and experiences?
- What values or beliefs do you hope others see in our group as we work with others who may or may not share the same values or beliefs we hold?

- What influence do you hope to have as a change agent? How do you hope to shape beliefs and thinking of others?
- Do any of your Key Influencers have ideas about the same topic that differ from what you do? What have you learned from the differing perspectives you've experienced from people you look up to and respect?
- What is key to taking in differing ideas and determining for yourself what YOU believe? (Note if not mentioned: listening, showing respect, staying curious, asking questions, seeking to understand, and looking at things from a different angle.)
- Are you willing to be open to differing beliefs, opinions, values, and perspectives of others? How can being open to hearing other perspectives be a sign of respect? How can it help you become a better change agent in the long run?

WHO AM I?

 20–25 minutes

 paper
writing utensils

DIRECTIONS Explain that their challenge is to create a poem about who
they really are. The key to creating this poem is to be able
to ask themselves one question for each prompt and then be able to
breathe, listen closely, and jot down answers as they come. It's that easy.

> ### Facilitator's Note
>
> For this activity you may need to incorporate more
> time to process depending on how you choose to
> close out the activity.

Read the poem together as a kicking off point.

Who am I?

Who am I?
This is the question I ask myself.
The answer easily comes.
I am a wife, a daughter, an aunt, and a sister.

Who am I?
I ask again.
I am a neighbor, an entrepreneur, a trainer, and
a leader.

Who am I?
Again, the answers flow. And my breathing is steady.
I am a writer, a coach, a sometimes gardener,
a stained-glass artist, a book lover, a crafter, a
meditator, and a dog lover.

Who am I?
I know these aspects well.
I am a listener, an encourager, a discerner, a friend,
and a helper.

Who am I?
This time my hand pauses and I take several deep
breaths stilling my rambling thoughts.
I ask again. Who am I?
I strain to hear my heart-centered voice within.

I am surprised to discover I really want to know.
I want to hear, need to hear, the voice of my being,
the reason for my heartbeat and presence on
this earth.

Who am I?
The answer comes, my Self is delighted to have
been asked.

I am a being made for joy.
I am born of God
and a gift to the world.
I am a powerful creator.
I am a joy bringer.
I am made for peace.
I delight in grace.
I radiate love.

I am light and dark and sunshine and shade.
I am growth and life and mistakes and little deaths.
And in all the seasons that make up my life,
I simply am abundantly, uniquely, imperfectly me.

And she is everything. I like her.

Susan G. Ragsdale

Have participants draw four vertical lines on a sheet of paper to create columns. They should title the first column "actions" then ask themselves "Who am I?", breathe deeply, and make a list of words or phrases that come to mind as they reflect on all the roles they've played in life or all the actions they've taken to express themselves. Give them 3 minutes.

Repeat this process for each column. Prompt them to keep breathing and asking, "Who am I?" as they write.

The 2nd column is "places and activities." As participants question and breathe, they should list the places and activities they do that make them smile, joyful, warm, happy, or feel alive.

Participants title the 3rd column "people and character." Here they jot down names of people who have been positive influences in their lives. They think too about what values are important to them.

The 4th column is dubbed "uniquely me." Invite the group to record the words or phrases that surface about the things that they like about themselves or that are particularly them.

Now, instruct them to weave together ideas from these different aspects of themselves into their own poem. Invite them to end their poem with a line or two that expresses the person they want to be, their most expanded, broadest, best self.

To close, you have options. You can ask the group for a few volunteers to share their poetry or talk about some of what they learned about themselves from this exercise. Or, you can have them break off into pairs or small groups to discuss, and then in the big group you can ask a few key questions to draw out the learning.

LEADERSHIP ASSOCIATIONS

 15–20 minutes

 index cards
writing utensils

DIRECTIONS Ask the group to think about leadership qualities. As they think, distribute index cards to each person. Explain that each person should write their answer (a component of good leadership) in large letters across the top of their index card and underline it.

Call time at 30 seconds, then have participants pass their cards clockwise to the person sitting next to them. The new cardholder will read the word they receive, then write beneath it the first word they think of that further refines or describes that component of leadership based on the word they see. For example, one person may write down *visionary*. The next person, upon seeing the word *visionary*, may write down *inspiring* beneath it.

Participants should continue passing cards clockwise until each original leadership quality has 4–5 associated words beneath it. Collect the cards, shuffle them, and choose one to give to a volunteer.

The volunteer's job is to try to get the group to guess the original word. They can weave the other words listed into a description or story. The words do not have to be used in the order they are written. The hard part? Each volunteer is playing against the clock to get the rest of the group to guess the word. (Allow 35–45 seconds.)

After playing, place the cards face-up in a central area so everyone can see everything the group associates with leadership. Build on their words. Discuss what makes a good leader and how they can—or do—exemplify the qualities they identified in this game.

Going Deeper

- How are you a leader personally?
- How would your peers say you are a leader? Which trait would they say that you have?

- In what ways do you take action in your neighborhood? School? Community? Work? Politics? In solving world issues?
- If you aren't taking action in these areas, what is one step you could take to put your leadership skills to work?

WHAT'S MY STYLE?

 5–15 minutes

 statements

DIRECTIONS ► Have the group vote with their feet to stand in an area of the room the leader points to for each descriptor that best portrays their response for each question.

What is your preference for getting work done?
- Independent: Like to work alone
- Group: Like to work with others
- Mixed: Sometimes like to work alone, sometimes like to work with others

When someone asks you a question, do you...
- Need time to think it through to give your best answer
- Respond easily off the top of your head
- Ask lots of questions to clarify before you speak

When you are facing fears or challenges, do you...
- Ask questions to think your way through what you'll do
- Instantly worry or get tied up in knots
- Get defensive and/or assume a combative stance
- Squarely face your fears and/or the unknown

When you are given a "thinking" assignment or task, do you need...
- White noise background or music
- Silence
- To write things out
- To brainstorm with drawings

What kind of action are you drawn to?
- Working with your hands
- Researching/reading/planning
- Interacting with others
- Expressing things creatively or through art

What is the environment that feels best for you to do good work?
- Very active
- Steady, quiet pace
- Variety: what you do changes a lot
- Chaos: never know what will happen

What is your work focus preference?
- Move from project to project
- Get good at 1–3 areas
- Multitask every day

What is your natural energy?
- Low energy
- High energy
- Energy flows up and down

If time allows, have the group do a moment of self-reflection and jot down a few notes about what they realized about themselves and what they know to be true about their preferred styles. Invite them to consider: *What characteristics, values, and preferences define your preferred style? What is ideal for you?*

After 1–2 minutes, have group members turn to a neighbor and share a little about their thoughts and how they can use that knowledge to work smarter as a leader.

Going Deeper

Tell the group: "Knowing yourself, your preferences and style can help you make better choices of where to invest your time and energy to have the greatest impact. If you like working with your hands (woodwork, tinkering with cars, gardening, etc.), then a service project in which you are sitting at a desk all day to answer the phone may not hold that much appeal. Knowing the answers to these questions can also help you make better choices in how you communicate when you're working on teams."

- Where have you seen your preferences line up naturally with what you are doing as a leader?
- Where has it been difficult?

- What could you do now, with your new self-awareness, to make any challenging situation work out better? How can you bring your best self to the table every time?
- Are there areas where you may need to have a conversation to ask for a different role? What are they? What do you need to ask for and how will that change help you lead better? How will the change help you serve better within the group?

LEADERSHIP CORNER CHOICES

 15 minutes

 statements

DIRECTIONS Explain that you will read aloud a statement along with four potential choices that match the four corners of the room. After all the options are read (with you pointing to each corner to match a choice), participants should move to the corner of the room that represents the answer that best fits their response.

After everyone has picked a corner, ask why people selected the answer they did.

 Facilitator's Note

Monitor time here. If you are running short of time, just have one or two participants speak for each corner choice. If answers are quick, you can have more people share. Woven into the assessment are some follow-up questions to dive a little deeper into thinking about their leadership styles.

Experiential Statements

The tool I most need to help me organize a project (my team) is a:
- Hammer
- Broom
- Wrench
- A kitchen mixer

If I were to describe myself as a leader, I would say I am a:
- Cruise ship
- Hot air balloon
- Bicycle
- Train

Ask: *What are the pluses of your particular way of leading? What are the minuses of your particular leadership style? What supporting styles do you need to harmonize who you are?*

When it comes to decision-making, you might think I am a:
- Hawk
- Dog
- Ant
- Giraffe

Ask: *How might your decision-making style impact others?*

When it comes to handling conflict, I'm a/an:
- Beaver
- Moth
- Ostrich
- Cat

When it comes to communicating with my teammates, you might say I'm most like a:
- Piece of Swiss cheese
- Instruction manual
- Measuring spoon
- Toaster

Ask: *In what situations does your communication style work best?*

Growing up, you could say my family's motto was:
- Time flies when you're having fun
- Haste makes waste
- Time is on my side
- Never put off to tomorrow what you can do today

Ask: *How has your family motto impacted the way you view and choose to spend your time?*

Wrap up this activity with a few remarks such as: "We have different frames of reference for how we complete tasks, communicate, and lead. Different isn't bad; it's just different. Start paying attention to the strengths and styles of your various group members. Look for ways to match teammates to leadership when the task best suits their leadership style."

THE LEADER IN ME

 10–20 minutes

 chart paper
markers

 Label chart paper pieces and stick around the room: *Step In,
Step Out, Walk It Out,* and *Step Up*

DIRECTIONS Set the stage: Leadership shows up in different ways. The
way you are involved in the community as a volunteer or
the way you participate in clubs are all opportunities for you to
demonstrate leadership. From a possible job perspective, employers
look at what you do or have done. From a personal perspective, you
are developing skills and figuring out what you're really passionate
about or interested in doing with your time, abilities and efforts.

Volunteering and leading show your ability to take initiative
and be responsible. Seizing opportunities to step up or step in show
the community that you've already been practicing and working on
cooperating with others, listening, communicating, and working
collaboratively toward goals. These skills are highly valued by
workplace teams as key to getting things done and running smoothly
as an agency.

Invite the group to think about the different ways they've shown
leadership at school, in the community, at their place of worship, in
after-school settings, or in previous jobs.

Point out the chart paper headings distributed around the room.
Briefly cover what each one means (defined below) to talk about the
different ways we lead.

Mini-lecture: The Different Ways We Lead

Step In: You demonstrate present-moment awareness and take action
in any given moment, leading with the gifts you can contribute.
Let's say you observe someone fumbling with bags of groceries and
trying to open a door. You instantly move to open the door or offer
to help hold the bags. Or, a crisis happens when a car's tire blows on
the interstate, and you pull over to see if everyone is okay or needs to

use your phone to call a tow truck. Or, you start the club meeting on time even though the club advisor isn't there yet. *Stepping in* calls for present-moment awareness and eyes wide open to choices one can make in the moment to act.

Step Out: Here, you are front and center, ahead of the pack. When a leader steps out, they move out of their comfort zone, take risks, and dare greatly. These are the individuals who take initiative and lead the way as they blaze a trail into unknown terrain without possibly knowing the results. Perhaps you start a brand-new initiative or club to address a community issue, or create a media campaign to educate others about the potential of all people in our community.

Walk It Out: You live in such a way that you are attentive to leading yourself well. Your influence expresses itself by your very example. You inspire others. Perhaps you decide to cultivate inner peace and dedicate time daily to meditative practices. Or, you actively work to treat everyone you meet with respect. Perhaps you commit to environmental stewardship, or you determine to reframe negative situations into positive ones. Your desire is to stay grounded in values that others experience in your very presence. Walking it out is a commitment to leading self and being the very best version of yourself every day. It is truly living by example.

Step Up: You decide you want to maximize the scope of your influence. In some cases, you might reach for formal or even volunteer positions of leadership. In these expanded capacities, you begin to manage others, a project, an idea, or even a vision. In this way, you may find yourself being the editor of the school paper, captain of the basketball team, or serving as a peer tutor or camp counselor. You might even recruit and oversee volunteers for the Special Olympics track team. Stepping up requires a commitment to managing and leading others.

Have the group breakoff into smaller teams and gather around the various leadership expressions to work together to jot down ideas for how each of them has led in that particular way. Rotate groups to a new chart every 2–3 minutes.

When done, look at all the various ways the participants have led. Celebrate their work to date.

Sum up with comments along these lines: Life, in its twists and curves, presents us with numerous opportunities to express our essential purpose and influence. The examples we just created illustrate the myriad of opportunities in life to express the leader within us. Every day we face choices. Every day we can use our essential connection to one another and to meaning and purpose to choose to lead well. We can be forces for good for ourselves, for our relationships, and for the world as a whole.

Our scope of influence may flow back and forth between the various steps of leadership moves. We may step in, step up, step out, or walk it out at different times in our lives. And that's okay. Some of us may choose to focus on one particular ripple effect that we want to serve as our prime directive. Others of us may choose to solely focus on living out a life of example, and that's okay. Doing the best we can with who we are wherever we are is the goal. We shine where we are.

Going Deeper

- Overall, what have you learned about yourself from your experience as a leader?
- What does it take to lead well?
- What have you learned about working with others?
- What have you learned about listening carefully? Communicating clearly?
- What have you learned about the importance of setting or holding out a vision?
- What have you learned about working hard to achieve your goal?
- What have you learned about working smart?
- How can you apply what you've learned and done well to future moments?
- How will remembering your experiences make you more sympathetic toward others who lead events or groups you are part of now? How can you use your leadership to be supportive of what they are doing?

Add-On

Want to go further? You can build in a conversation around skills. What are the skills used in each leadership expression? Chart their answers, then have the group sort them out by these classifications—

- I've used this skill before in previous experiences.
- This skill is totally new to me.
- This skill is one I want to work on.
- I've recently gained or practiced this skill, and it has strengthened what I knew I could do.

To Go Before

According to various dictionaries, the origin of the word *leader* is "to go before as a guide"—like Yoda. And to be a guide or leader, you need to know things about yourself and where you're going. That understanding brings us around to the fact that our intentions, choices, words, and actions all have an impact. But are we consciously and thoughtfully aware of what we're choosing?

I AM A LEADER

 15–20 minutes

 paper
writing utensils

DIRECTIONS Divide the group into smaller teams of 3–6. Distribute paper and writing utensils. Ask each team to vertically write the words I AM A LEADER. For each letter of this acrostic, they should think about a quality, value, skill, or attitude they personally have that can fit each letter. What makes them desirable as a leader? Why should/would businesses, groups, or organizations want them on their team? How do they lead already with family, peers, or in the activities they are part of? Give them 5 minutes to work.

Next, give teams 3 minutes work together to create a 30-second commercial to promote themselves as a group as the leaders they already are. When time is up, take turns having teams perform their creation.

Going Deeper

- What did you learn about yourself from doing this activity?
- Was there a trait you identified that surprised you? If so, what was it?
- What attributes do you think most employers value the most?
- What quality do you feel is your strongest as a leader? As a potential employee? Are the two the same? Why or why not?
- What strength do you have that you feel is unique to you?
- How will your particular skill set add to wherever you are, at home, at school, at work or as a volunteer? What do you bring that will enhance/add/improve any group you're part of?
- What strengths stand out as ones we share as a group?
- How can we leverage our strengths and talents to make a difference in _____ (fill in the blank: X project? As a club? Etc.)

POWER UP!

 5–20 minutes

 colored paper
markers
tape

(optional)   Create a list of core leadership or personal skills your group is focused on building. What do you want them to gain on the tail end of being in your space? No idea? Look at the skills listed in the **Strengths Walk** activity on page 40 to spark thoughts.

Make signs on colored paper and post around the room:

- *Superhero Strong:*   I Use This Skill a Lot
- *Sidekick Strong:*   I Am More Powerful When I Have a Superhero to Work With
- *Fan Strong:*   Look Up in the Air! Those Skills Seem SO Far Away!

DIRECTIONS ▶   Using the chosen skills, have participants honestly rank themselves on how powerful they are with each skill's usage. As you call out a skill, participants will "vote" with their feet by going to stand under the sign that best fits their response.

Explain the different signs:

- *Superhero Strong:* I Use This Skill a Lot (Define: Youth feel really confident using this skill.)
- *Sidekick Strong:* I Am More Powerful When I Have a Superhero to Work With (Define: Youth are actively working on this skill and value guidance.)
- *Fan Strong:* Look Up in the Air! Those Skills Seem SO Far Away! (Define: Youth can't even imagine being able to use this skill.)

Option: In addition to standing under signs or instead of, have the group assume the appropriate pose to go with each stance:

- *Superhero Strong:* Participants raise both arms above their heads and sway them back and forth like they're flying
- *Sidekick Strong:* Participants stand with their feet hip width apart, place their hands on their hips, and turn their heads to look proudly off to one side
- *Fan Strong:* Participants point one finger up in the air and look in that direction (like drawing attention to a superhero flying in the air)

After talking through each sign and what it means, do a practice run for them to vote with their feet. Ask: "Where's your power when it comes to staying calm when something goes wrong or not according to plan? Are you Superhero Strong and stay outwardly calm all the time? Sidekick Strong and maybe stay calm with coaching/reminders? Or Fan Strong and you think it's a great skill to have but can't imagine being able to stay calm when things go wrong?"

Instruct them to go stand under the power level sign that best fits how they feel.

Work through several skills. When desired, after the group has sorted themselves around a particular skill, ask for those in the Superhero Strong stance to share 1 or 2 tips with the others to help them develop these super power muscles.

Tip: If you know your group well and you think they are better at a skill than they are giving themselves credit for, point out how you've seen them use a skill specifically.

Going Deeper

- Which skills do you think are your strongest?
- What skills do you think this group most needs from you?
- What skills do you need to work on? Why those skills?
- Which skills are most relevant for being the leader you want to be?
- How can we help one another further develop our super powers?

Variation

This game can be played using all the skills you want to cover in one session or in multiple sessions; it can also be adapted to be used as an icebreaker to introduce a topic that needs to be covered.

SELF-TWISTER

 15–20 minutes

 statements

DIRECTIONS, Have the group stand. Explain that they are going to do a personal assessment of their emotional, spiritual, and mental habits by playing Self-Twister.

Do a practice round with this sample statement to illustrate how it works: *Everyone who has a pet, tap your right foot.*

Explain that with each statement read, if it applies to them, they must do the prescribed action and keep doing it even when adding on new actions or until instructed otherwise.

Instruct them to quit tapping their foot. Now, start the assessment:

- If anyone has ever struggled with making a decision of some kind, place your left hand on top of your head. (Keep it there)
- If anyone has ever felt a conflict between pleasing someone else and doing what was right for yourself, place your right hand on the left side of your waist.
- If anyone has ever had your emotions "triggered" by a situation and not responded in a way you want to respond, crunch your elbows in toward each other.
- If anyone has ever been in an uncomfortable situation where you felt you had to pick between conflicting values (for example, lie to someone because you don't want to hurt their feelings or be honest and know you'll hurt their feelings), then cross your left foot over your right one.
- If anyone has ever mentally beaten themselves up for making a mistake, doing the wrong thing or had any kind of negative self-talk, then rock your upper body back-and-forth from the waist.

Say: "Try to hold your position as you look around at each other. Look at what we've done to ourselves! This uncomfortable position is one of our making. It was our thoughts, our negative talk. We're the creators behind all of that, no one else. That means WE can undo it. We can *choose* how to respond to triggers, struggles and life around us. We have power, a loving, supportive power within us to help us face life with grace and ease."

How can we untangle from our self-inflicted twister? Let's try now:

- Everyone who deliberately takes time for quiet or solitude, stop rocking.
- Everyone who questions something told you by another and digs with critical questions to determine the truth of the matter, uncross your feet, and stand balanced.
- Everyone who takes time to meditate, pray or engage in a spiritual practice, open up your elbows.
- Everyone who spends time in nature: taking a walk, sitting in the grass, staring at a cloud or tree, or smelling a flower, then drop your right hand from your waist.
- Everyone who does a body scan to see where stress is felt and then deliberately relaxes that area, or starts taking deep breaths to relax, then drop your left hand down.
- Everyone who journals, does art, or plays on a regular basis, sit down.
- Everyone who makes it a practice to express gratitude for all that is good in your life, smile or if you are still twisted in some way, drop the twist and sit down, too.

Conclude with some closing remarks such as: Every day there is chatter in our heads, our minds endlessly produce thoughts, thousands of thoughts. And we're surrounded by external noises: the bings, beeps, bells, and chimes of social media and technology; the commercials and advertisements of marketing that bombard us with messages to buy this or go here in order to find peace, have fun, or get rest.

BUT, the truth is we have within us the ability to go within, connect mind, body, and spirit together as a powerhouse of flexible, calm, balanced centeredness that will help us deal with all the twisting, turbulent emotions, thoughts, and actions we face as we go through our day.

Going Deeper

- What healthy practices do you regularly do to take care of your own well-being?
- Did we name any practices you'd like to try? Which one(s) and why?

- What other strategies do you have for dealing with noisy, stormy thoughts even "triggers?"
- Do you believe you have power in your own life? Power to make choices with intention, choose the attitudes you want to have or cultivate the spirit you desire? Why or why not?
- What are some choices you can make today that will impact the kind of person you want to be?

SHAZAM! BA ZING GA! GOTCHA!

 20–35 minutes

 writing utensil
paper
3–4 markers
chart paper

DIRECTIONS: Ask the group how they would define the word "triggers" when it refers to someone responding in a certain way to a given situation.

If not brought up, point out that as human beings, we can develop over time certain reactive responses to a given circumstance. We call the situation a "trigger" because it activates within us a set, instant response that we don't even think about. We just react.

(If desired, show the *Homer Simpson* clip of "Ow! Quit it. Ow! Quit it.")

> **Facilitator's Note**
>
> The use of the term "trigger" can be tricky. All of us have them. All of us need to be aware of them. The purpose of this activity is for self-awareness to identify what we can do to manage our own emotions and come up with positive ways to respond when we are accidentally or intentionally triggered.

Mini-lecture

Explain that cells in our brain talk to each other (the communication system is through the synapsis). The more frequently the cells talk to each other, the stronger and faster their communication signal becomes.

With "triggers," you have a scenario that sets off the established communication lines and you respond in the same way that you have in the past—even when you don't want to.

The good news is that we can change our patterns by inputting new information and disrupting the flow. We DECIDE how we will respond since we know, for example, that our baby sister is always going to come up and pinch us in the arm. She's been doing it for years because we've always responded with "ouch!" and gotten angry, which, as is usually the case with siblings, only encourages her to keep pinching because she likes getting under your skin.

Since you know she's going to pinch you and you don't want to get angry, you decide in advance HOW you'll respond when she pinches you. You change the pattern to one where you are in control of what you do, and you can be happy with yourself for how you choose to respond.

That's how the brain works. So, the "pinch" now becomes a signal for "Hey! Do that reaction you decided you want to do instead of how you've always responded."

The planned interruption works, but it takes practice. The more you do it; the more you choose your response, the more you start building up your new communication system in your brain and the happier you will be.

Don't expect that you will immediately stop your sister from pinching you, but you will change how you respond and that's a big step. And quite possibly, she may back away after several failed attempts to get you angry because it's no longer fun.

Triggers Identification Group Work

Let's brainstorm different triggers, little things that annoy us, or maybe it's the everyday things that make us lose our patience. Chart ideas from the group.

When done, point out the magic markers on hand and instruct each person that they have three votes to cast. They should place a dot next to the trigger idea or ideas they want to further explore. They can cast all three votes on one idea or spread them around with two here and one there or choose three different ideas all together.

Once everyone has voted, count up the votes and pick the top 2–4 trigger ideas for groups to work on. Write one trigger heading on the top of each piece of chart paper.

Divide the group into smaller teams of 2–4. Give each team one of the triggers and have them brainstorm and record different ways to disrupt that trigger to respond in a positive way. Give two minutes to work.

If time permits, have groups rotate the triggers and let each group brainstorm more ideas for two minutes on their new trigger. Repeat rotation as many times as desired in the time you have.

Time Your Trigger Response, Then Stop

Dr. Eli Parrot shared with me a tool she uses with young people to handle worry and fretting—which are other triggers that can spiral us into a place we don't want to go. She tells her clients:

Set a worry time. Every day at 8:00, for example, you can worry as much as you want for 10–15 minutes, but then you're done. When the thoughts come back, remind them that you'll revisit them tomorrow at the set time. You're training your brain to create a healthy pattern to focus and then let go appropriately rather than being consumed by a worry. You may even get to a point where you don't need to worry at all.

I would also add that, as mentors, we must also manage our own anxieties and not let our stuff spew onto others. Instead, as mentors, we bring the focus right back to them: supporting, focusing, asking questions, helping them think through consequences of their actions, and affirmation.

Practice

Have the group self-select partners. Give everyone two minutes to brainstorm the code word or image each of them wants to use whenever they are personally triggered. Explain that when a trigger happens, it is now a "bat signal" for help to come (in the form of their newly identified action). Their new signal can be a warrior yell, or a code word like "Shazam" to indicate they are tapping into their superhero self. Or, their signal can be factual like "Not Gonna Happen" or humorous like Sheldon's "Ba Zin Ga." It can be whatever it is that is unique to them that they will remember. And hopefully make them laugh (which will help break the cycle of triggers).

After two minutes, have one participant in each pair share a trigger from the group brainstorm. The other partner should give his "bat signal" indicator, then share how he wants to respond to that trigger.

Switch and let the other partner have their turn.

Going Deeper

- What are some of the "bat signals" you created?
- What triggers do you struggle with the most?
- What actions would you like to take to respond to those triggers? How are you going to tap your superhero self and make a change?

Add-On

Have participants write down on an index card their email address (or however you keep in contact with your group), a trigger, their new "bat signal" to save the day, and the specific response they want to take when triggered.

Collect the index cards and send them an email in 1 month to ask if they are using their new "bat signal" and encourage them to keep practicing their new strategies.

COMFORT LEVELS

 20–30 minutes

 none

DIRECTIONS ▸ Say something like it is a given that we will encounter people or situations that are new to us. Maybe they catch us by surprise or are different from us. Or, maybe we're in a city, part of town, state, or country that we've never visited before. Life is full of diversities. How comfortable are you with difference? We're going to explore several scenarios and see how comfortable we feel initially in these various situations.

Teach the group the three levels of comfort in conflict and the actions that go with each level. The three levels are comfortable, risk, and danger.

When a statement is read and you feel "comfortable" in this situation, simply walk in place. You got this. You are comfortable doing this.

When the statement read is about something you can do but it's a bit of a stretch for you, then indicate that by "stretching" out your hands above your head or to the side.

If the scenario doesn't feel comfortable at all, then crunch your body inward toward your stomach mimicking a "protective stance."

 Facilitator's Note

We never know when triggers will occur. Or how extensive their impact is. Sometimes we may unknowingly step on an emotional landmine. Past abuse or trauma memories might arise.

Remember that you are the safe space. Emulate safety, know your group, and give yourself permission to change scenarios or statements if you know something will be an issue. Know, too, what options your workplace offers for trauma-informed care.

Go over the three levels again having the group perform the action for each: comfortable, risk, and danger.

Do a practice statement with the group: You're asked to walk across a swinging bridge and it's windy. Do you feel comfortable doing that? Or, is it a bit of a stretch but you're willing to risk and do it? Or, is your initial reaction that there is no way you'd cross that bridge because it feels dangerous?

Experiential Statements

- A child you don't know runs up to you in the grocery store and wraps his arms around your legs in a big hug and won't let go. How do you initially feel?
- After giving a homeless man a dollar, he leans into your car against the window to keep talking. How comfortable are you?
- While visiting a nursing home, a resident grabs your hand and simply holds on, long enough that you need her to let go of your hand so that you can move on. How comfortable are you?
- In delivering food to people who are homeless on a street corner, one handicapped woman indicates that she wants to give you a kiss on the mouth. How comfortable are you?
- A stranger gets into your personal space while waiting for the bus and begins a loud conversation with you. How comfortable are you?
- You suddenly realize that the person sitting next to you on the plane that you thought was a girl is not. How comfortable are you?
- During the day, a stranger approaches you at the gas pump and asks if he can ask you a question. He launches into his story and wants money. How comfortable are you?
  - What if this scene took place at night? How comfortable would you be?
  - What if you didn't see him coming and your first indication of his presence was when he tapped you on the shoulder? How comfortable would you be?

- You call to upgrade your phone and the person on the other end has a heavy accent. How comfortable are you?
- You are working on a project and have been paired with someone from a different country who barely speaks your language. How comfortable are you?

Wrap Up

We have different comfort levels with challenging situations. Here we looked at the social and emotional settings. Part of our discomfort is because of our own moral code, or how we grew up and our beliefs, or how our opportunities to engage with people different from us have shaped us.

There will be times when we aren't comfortable for whatever reason. We have signals in our bodies if we pay attention. Our necks tighten, our shoulders hunch, a pain stabs in our gut, side, or back, or we quit breathing! All of these occurrences are signs of stress. These moments can move us from social-emotional awareness to management of our emotions. They can also be signals to move toward empathy and seeking to understand the other person's perspective by getting into their shoes.

Going Deeper

- What can help set us at ease in new situations or when meeting new people?
- How can we help set others at ease?
- It is a given that there will be times when we aren't comfortable, for whatever reason. How can we ensure that we don't have knee-jerk negative reactions? How can we ensure the actions we take are ones of our choosing?
- How can we embrace our discomfort? How can we stretch ourselves to learn, grow, and still be kind and respectful, treating others as we want to be treated?
- How can we look for the opportunities in uncomfortable situations? How can we focus on what is good and beautiful?

VALUES COMPASS

 15–25 minutes

 writing utensils
sticky notes
index cards

DIRECTIONS ▸ Ask the group to reflect on some of the highs and lows in their lives; times when they excelled, times when they faced challenges, and even times when they failed. When they think about their lives, what are some of the values they see at play in those moments? For example, loyalty? Responsibility? Caring? Honesty? Fairness?

Invite the participants to jot down one value per sticky note. Give them 1–2 minutes to reflect. Then, prompt with more question: What do you want people to see in you? What do you want people to associate with your character? What do you want your family to say you have? Your friends? Employers? What other values are important to you?

Give another 1–2 minutes for them to reflect and write.

Prompt again: What are values that keep you on target for the type of leader you want to be (in conflict, during growth of a program, or while things go well)? What do you take with you wherever you go? Is it a love of kids? Of nature? Of family? Faith? Creativity? Compassion? What?

Discuss together thoughts and remind them to jot down on their sticky notes any new values that come to mind that they personally want as part of their lives.

Now, ask participants to spread out and look at all the values they've recorded. Invite them to think about what their core guiding values are—the ones that no matter what, THESE are the ones that drive their decisions, actions, and words. Ask them to narrow down their different values to the 4 most important ones. Give them 30 seconds or so to do this.

Congratulate the group for determining the values that will serve, at least for now, as their guiding compass. Have them draw a simple compass on an index card and place a value at each of the four points of the compass: N, S, E, and W. Remind them that a compass lets them know where true north is at all times. They should record their highest guiding value on the northern tip This value should be the one that fits this description: "Without this in place, nothing else matters."

Invite participants to keep their compass in a place they can return to time and again when they are faced with difficult decisions. They can carry it in their wallet, post it on a wall, or tape it inside a notebook. This activity may be one they'll visit again and again over the years as they continue to grow, learn, and expand their leadership heart.

Going Deeper

- What are your five core values? How did you whittle it down to these five?
- Can you think of a time when a situation or person challenged your values? How did you resolve it?
- What helps you stick with these most important values when someone else wants you to live by their values?

Add-On

Invite participants to post their values compass in a prominent place where they'll see it often. They can read their values out loud daily as an affirmation. "Today I will be guided by my desire to be loving, honest, helpful, loyal, and fair." They can refer to the values compass when making decisions and determine to live by what will make them a person of integrity, thus living with intention. For example, "When I have conflict with someone, I intend to let them know I value the relationship over the conflict. We will work out the disagreement, and I will be respectful through the process."

Option two: Stick the values together creating a sticky flipbook to keep on hand or make a smaller version of the values compass and place it in their wallet next to their driver's license.

STEPPING OUT MY VALUES

 15–20 minutes

 none

DIRECTIONS ▸ Say: Arnold Schwarzenegger in the movie *Conan The Barbarian* is asked the question, "What is best in life?" Conan was very clear on his goal, what he was about, and the values that guided his course. While not the values we uphold, it's still fun to hear his voice and passion answering the question.

The point is that life is smoother when we know and live from our personally identified core guiding values. Then, when we face challenges or run into situations where values may bump, we can intentionally make decisions that reflect what we care about most.

We're going to spend some time thinking about our lives and what guides us. What values are important to you? Which ones do you live by or want to live by?

Ask the participants to stand in a straight line. Explain that you will read them a scenario and they should take one step to the left or the right depending on which answer matches what they would do. Remind them to think about what value might be behind each decision.

To make it easy, always indicate the left side for the first answer choice and the right side for the second answer. Once everyone has made their selection, direct them to return to center. **Going Deeper** questions are woven in throughout the activity as prompts for further discussion.

Scenarios

You see someone ahead of you throw a plastic bottle on the ground. Take one step to the left if you would pick the bottle up. Take one step to the right if you wouldn't.

Ask: *Would any of you say something to the person? What would you say? Is there a way to say something nicely and to prompt them to think about what they just did?*

***

Your two best friends had a huge argument and are no longer speaking. You've heard both sides. Do you take a side or try to maintain your own good relationship with both letting them know that the argument is theirs, not yours? Step to the left if you take a side and step to the right if you stay out of it.

Ask: *How do you decide when you need to speak up or when to stay silent?*

***

Shirley spent hours in the kitchen making a homemade meal. It's lasagna. You hate lasagna. Do you eat it (showing love and appreciation for her efforts) or do you let her know you don't like lasagna but still appreciate her work (honesty)? Step to the left if you eat it and step to the right if you don't.

Ask: *What do you do when values bump? In this case, it's love vs. honesty. How do you decide which value to live out? Or is there a way to honor both values?*

***

You've been offered a new job. You will make more money, but the job isn't something you'd like doing. If you take the job, step left. If you don't take the job, step to the right.

Ask: *Why did you make the choice you did? What values are at play in this decision?*

***

A protest rally for something you believe in is happening two blocks from where you live on a day you're free and at just the perfect time. Step left if you attend. Step right if you don't.

Ask: *What changes do you actively support in your life? How?*

Live and Lead by Example

We can *walk it out* to live by example—being kind to everyone, demonstrating a commitment to recycling, or taking time to hear all sides to every argument. Finally, we can *step up* to lead in both formal and informal positions, paid or volunteer. Leadership positions in after-school programs, service clubs, places of faith, or school clubs are all places where we (youth or adult!) can serve and lead—organizing a food drive, helping canvas neighborhoods during elections, or creating design sets for a play.

STINKY SITUATIONS

 15–25 minutes

 none

DIRECTIONS Explain that we can find ourselves in situations that aren't very fun. The circumstances may even be undesirable, and a choice may have to be made to move forward or make a change. For each scenario read, the group will rank each one by one of three choices using their thumbs as a thumb-o-meter to indicate their reaction.

Have the group mirror your thumb movements as you explain them:

Thumbs up means "I can make this work. I can go with it."

Thumbs sideways (held out horizontally) means "It's not great. It's not ideal, but I can perhaps make this work."

Thumbs down means "This stinks. This would be horrible for me."

 Facilitator's Note

Adapt the scenarios to fit your situation and group. For example, if your group is going to do a service-learning project, your scenarios can include situations and issues the group might face.

Scenarios

You are working with another student on a project who knows less than you do about how to get the project done but they insist on their answer. Your grade depends on the "group" work.

***

You are working for a boss who knows less than you do about how to get the job done and they don't listen to you.

***

You are working for or with someone who takes all the credit for work you did.

***

You are working somewhere when it becomes obvious they only want you there as a "token" to illustrate their commitment to X people group. You have no influence in your position.

***

You have an equal position to someone else. Your jobs are the same, but they get paid more.

***

You are part of a club where trust is low. Everyone is doing their own thing and not concerned about the group.

***

You are part of a group where viewpoints are so extreme that the group can't get anything done due to all the divisiveness.

***

You are working for a place that serves others and yet more money seems to be spent on upper management salaries than on actually meeting the needs of others.

Going Deeper

- Which scenario is the worst case possible? You'd hate it? (Recap each of the scenarios if need be.) Why?
- What could we do to reframe it and make it better? What ideas do we have?
- Which scenarios have you experienced? What did you do to make it better? Or what do you wish you had done?
- What do we have control over? (Say if not said by the group, "How we respond!")
- Why is it important to dig in and tap our values when we're faced with challenges? What difference does that make?

Our Power

We all have an impact. We speak. Or not. We act. Or not. And those choices exert ripples of influence. Every time. The only questions then are: Are we intentionally choosing what we do? How far reaching is our effect going to be? And how far do we want to expand (and expend) our power?

VALUE WHAT?

 15–25 minutes

 chart paper
markers

DIRECTIONS Start off by stating the idea that **value conflict is a difference of opinion created by differences in long-held beliefs and world views.** The conflict cannot be easily resolved with facts because the disagreements are based on closely held beliefs, not facts.

Ask the group what they think of what was said. Ask them to give examples of conflicts they've read, seen, heard or experienced that were about beliefs and how people view the world.

From the discussion or from prompts, ask for volunteers to take on roles of supporting two different sides of a given scenario. They should each express what they think the belief, world view, and opinion is. They have 1 minute each.

Chart their answers. Monitor to keep things reflective and learning instead of heated. When each one is done, ask the group to contribute more to each side of the value conflict.

Switch prompts and volunteers and repeat process then discuss.

Prompts

- Education should be affordable and accessible for everyone, maybe even free.
- Everyone can have a good future. They just have to work for it.
- The minimum wage should be fair, livable wage that reflects living expenses.
- Our country should take care of its weakest members (the elderly, the sick, the disabled, and the neglected.)
- All people groups should have the same rights.
- Switching to sustainable energy is important in order to be environmentally responsible.
- If there is a job that requires a certain skill set, then the pay for that skill set should be the same amount no matter if it's a woman or man who does the work. Same work, same pay.

- You want to get married in a church, but your fiancé has a friend who is willing to get an online certification to perform the marriage
- You are at a protest that is getting heated and the police may start arresting people.
- You see someone being treated unfairly and pull out your phone to start recording. You're noticed and negative attention comes your way.

Going Deeper

- What underlying values do you see in each side of the conflict? (Do this one prompt at a time.)
- What values are the same? What differs?
- Have you ever held a belief that you found out later was wrong? How difficult was it to let go of your belief?
- What about your world view? How has that changed over time for you?
- Are values wrong? (No.)
- How do we, then, learn to disagree peacefully when our values conflict?
- How can we be open to different perspectives without feeling the need to dub one right and the other wrong?
- Why do you think we turn values differences into being right or wrong?
- Why do we struggle with accepting that other people have different experiences and understanding of how things work than we do?
- How might listening, asking questions, and taking in other people's experiences enrich our own understanding of the world?
- How can we actively show respect for other points of view? What actions can we take moving forward?

DIVERSITY WHAT?

 15–25 minutes

 writing utensils
index cards

 Look up and record the dictionary definition of diversity on an index card.

DIRECTIONS▸ Say: Diversity means different things to different people. If you asked a 3rd grader what the word means, you would get a completely different definition than if you ask a 70-year-old. The experience—or lack thereof—colors everyone's understanding of diversity in a substantial way. Those different filters can create frustration and miscommunication even when it's caring individuals who are trying to craft a training or experience To offset that frustration and miscommunication, we want to explore how we all understand diversity.

Divide the group into teams of 3–4. Distribute writing utensils and index cards. Give them 15 minutes to discuss diversity and craft how they would define it. Each team should write their team name (or contributor names) on their definition.

 Facilitator's Note

If time, put all the definitions out for the group to see. *How can they build in elements of the different definitions into their definition? What do they want to keep? What do they want to see? What describes diversity at its very best?* Adding this step to the process helps build off of each person's ideas and experiences and contributes to synergy.

When time is up, collect all the definitions. Discretely, add in the official one.

Tell the group that you are going to read each definition one at a time, and participants should vote for what they think is the official definition of diversity. Allow 1–2 minutes for teams to discuss after having read all the choices. After revealing the real definition, applaud choices that got the most vote and any teams who may have guessed the standard definition.

Going Deeper

- How does the "official" definition resonate with you? Does it fit your idea or experience of diversity?
- Is it inclusive? Does it leave anything out? If so, what?
- What was common to our various understandings of diversity?
- What, if anything, surprised you to hear?
- What can we agree on as our understanding of diversity?
- What aspects do we want to honor?
- What aspects do we need to take a harder look at and work on to reach understanding and mutual respect?
- What tips can we give others to help them embrace and value diversity?

FORCED CHOICES

 15–20 minutes

 paper
writing utensils
selected issue perspectives

 Make and post the following signs equidistance around
the space:

- Gender/Sexual Identity/Sexual Orientation
- Race/Ethnicity/Skin Color
- Mental Capabilities/Physical Abilities/Emotional Maturity
- Social Class/Education Level
- Religion/Spirituality, Personal Belief System
- Citizenship/Immigration Status/Language
- Age/Maturity/Wisdom
- Coolness/Fitting In/Popularity

DIRECTIONS, Explain that various aspects of identity have been coupled with other aspects on the signs around the room. This was done to make it a safer activity for individuals to keep their focus inward and more on their own identity. Some combinations may seem related and others will not. Regardless of the pairings, participants should stand underneath the sign that has the best choice (the one that fits best) as they respond to statements that will be read aloud. Explain that this is a silent exercise of self-awareness. Ask them to respect one another's responses. Acknowledge the diversity of how participants look and experience their own identity. There are no cookie cutter molds.

After each statement is read and people have self-selected their response, ask them to regroup in the center of the room. Remind them frequently to keep their focus inward on themselves as they reflect on how their own identity has been shaped.

Continue through as many statements as you want to cover. Conversation prompts are woven throughout where you can pause to let participants turn to a neighbor to share or ask for a few volunteers to speak up within the bigger group.

Experiential Statements

- I think about this aspect of my identity the most
- I think about this aspect of my identity the least
  - Why is that so?
- This part of my identity has the most effect on how people treat me
  - How does this part of your identity have the most effect on how people treat you?
- This was the most emphasized in my family
- This was the least emphasized in my family
  - How was it not emphasized? What was?
- This aspect of my identity is most new to me
- I feel most discomfort about this part of my identity
- I have had my most rewarding experiences with this aspect of my identity
- I learned my most painful lessons from this part of my identity
  - Would you change that part of your identity if you could? Why?

- I feel extremely good about this aspect of my identity
  - Step forward if you are still working on this aspect of your identity
  - Ask for a few volunteers to share both from those who stepped forward and from those who did not step forward.

Going Deeper

- What was this process like for you?
- How do your feelings about these different aspects of your identity impact you?
- What were some of the things that came up for you? (If needed, repeat some of the statements to begin this dialogue.)
- How do these aspects of identity impact how you interact with others?
- What if anything, did you notice about the group overall?

STORYTELLING

 15–20 minutes

 Story prompts—1 per group

 Make copies of these story prompts (or ones you create) to distribute 1 per team.

Meal Time: Tell a story about a time you were at the dinner table. What are you eating? What does it smell like, taste like, look like? Where did you sit at the table? Who sat on either side of you? A family member? A friend? Where was your place? What meal are you eating? Is it a special event, a "pizza" Friday (or something else you had every Friday)? Or is it simply a school night with nothing special going on? What do you talk about at the table? Or do you?

***

Chores: Tell a story about the chores you do in the family. What do you do? Do you do this chore alone or with someone else? Do you have to be told to do it or do you just do it? Are there any sensory sensations you associate with this chore like soapy water, warmth from dried clothes, the buzz or the vacuum, or a lingering lemony scent? Are you rushing to get done? Is company coming? Is it spring cleaning and you're doing more than you usually do? Do you sing, listen to music, television, or talk while you work? How does it feel when you're done?

***

Weekend fun: Tell a story about what's fun for you on the weekend. What is it you look forward to on a Saturday afternoon? Are you outside or indoors? What do you do? Who is with you? Is this a special event or something you do frequently? What emotions do you associate with doing this activity? Are there scents? Tastes? Particular feelings? Or visuals that come to mind? What about how you feel inside when you recall or anticipate doing this fun moment?

***

DIRECTIONS Explain that the group is going to tell stories to each other as a way to work on their communication skills, reflect on their own experiences, and listen to other people's stories.

Invite them to reflect on great stories they have experienced recently in class, or from movies, books, TV shows, and so forth. Then, ask them to reflect on the elements that made their experience a great story.

Reiterate that a story has a beginning, a middle and an end. A story has momentum. It has to go somewhere and moves from one point to another.

Divide participants into small groups of 3–4. After giving each group a topic (it's okay if they have the same one), instruct them to read it aloud, then take turns telling their stories. Give them one minute per person.

Announce when groups should start and keep track of time. Signal groups at the end of a minute to let them know when the next person's turn is to share.

Repeat process until everyone has had an opportunity to be a storyteller.

Going Deeper

- What was this experience like for you?
- What part was hardest or easiest? Thinking of a story, telling your story, or listening to other people's stories? Why?
- What's the difference between hearing and listening?
- Have you ever become aware that you were using your "listening time" to decide what you were going to say when it became your turn instead of really focusing on what the other person was saying?
- How well did you feel you understood what the other person was saying? If you had questions or didn't understand something, how comfortable were you in seeking clarification?
- What indications did the group give that they were really listening to you tell your story?
- Why is reflecting on our own stories important?
- What can we learn from our own experiences? From others?
- How might paying attention to stories—ours and others—help us be better leaders?

RED CARPET CONVERSATIONS

 20–25 minutes

 notepad
writing utensils

DIRECTIONS Remind the group that stories have a beginning, a middle and an end. They also have momentum. They start at one point and go somewhere. They take you on a journey.

When we listen to others tell stories, we can sometimes help them enrich their own stories by asking curious questions. A curious question is a question that you can't know the answer to. You have no idea what the storyteller will answer, and you aren't trying to interject yourself into the story by creating an opportunity for you to say what YOU would do. You keep the focus on the other person and what's going on with their story.

"What happened next? What did you feel? What bus did you take to get to the ball field? What college are you thinking of attending?" are all samples of curious questions.

Whereas, *"How mad were you?"* is not an example of a curious question because it assumes and projects onto the person what you thought they felt (which probably means you would have felt that way in the same situation).

Ask for any questions, then divide participants into two equal groups. The first group sits in a circle facing outward 2 arms-length apart (at least, far enough from the other pairs so that they won't be easily distracted by other conversations). The second group creates a circle around the first group facing toward them so that participants are in pairs and sitting across from each other with a partner.

The inner circle is comprised of the people who are a **Celebrity You.** The outer circle is comprised of the **Reporters.** Make sure Reporters have pen and paper.

Each Celebrity You will have "red carpet treatment" and have 2 minutes to share their life story. Remind them that this is a snapshot. They might want to only highlight a current event or an important moment in their lives. Each Reporter takes down notes and asks curious questions to pull out more content.

After time is up, have the outer circle of Reporters rotate to the left one person to meet a new Celebrity You and get their story. Again, time the conversation for 2 minutes.

Repeat the process 1 more time.

After 3 rotations, have the groups switch spots in the circle. Reporters now become Celebrity You's and Celebrity You's become Reporters.

Continue process of storytelling and questions for 3 more rotations.

Going Deeper

Ask the Celebrity You's

- What was it like to tell your story?
- How did your story change as you kept telling it? Did you embellish it? Shorten it? Tell a different aspect?
- Did you feel listened to and supported?
- What signaled interest and support to you as you spoke?

Ask the Reporters

- What types of questions did you ask?
- Did your questions get broader or more detailed as you continued to ask more questions?
- What made you curious about the stories you heard?

Ask Everyone

- Were there any common themes to the stories shared and heard?
- What stories stood out from all those you heard?
- What, if anything, did you learn from telling your own story to someone else?
- What can you learn from this activity about the importance of listening and focusing on another and giving them "red carpet treatment?"

2 MYTHS & A TRUTH

 15–20 minutes

 paper
writing utensils

DIRECTIONS ▶ Distribute supplies and invite each person to think about the assumptions they've encountered about who they are based on their culture. Note that sometimes people make judgments that extend to a whole group of individuals or a whole family who share that culture.

Instruct the group: On your paper, write down 2 myths or assumptions and 1 truth about your culture as it plays out for yourself or in your family or the community you consider yourself a part of. Have 1 myth be something you hear said frequently and 1 myth be an assumption you've personally encountered. They can be about your culture, yourself, or your family. And for the truth, jot down 1 thing you wish others knew about you, your family, or culture.

Instruct the participants to put a star or asterisk beside the truth they have written. Each sentence should be written in fact form because the statements will be read aloud and the rest of the group will try to guess which of the three statements is true. For example: 1) I speak Spanish. 2) I eat tacos every day. 3) I will have a quinceañera for my 15th birthday.

After all the guesses, the person might comment in response, "My grandparents are from Mexico but I grew up in North Carolina. I only speak English. No, I don't eat tacos every day and that isn't even funny when people make that comment anymore. So numbers 1 and 2 are assumptions. Number 3 is the truth! I am very much looking forward to celebrating my birthday party."

Give participants 3 minutes to think and write answers, then collect all of the cards. Randomly read cards to the group, letting them guess which statement is the truth. After guesses, reveal which are myths or assumptions, then reiterate the true facts. Allow time for the author to make any further comments about what they have written.

Going Deeper

- What has been your experience of encountering assumptions about who you are because of your culture or ethnic background? How have you experienced misperceptions?
- What responses work best to counter misperceptions in a peaceful way?
- What myths or assumptions would you like to dispel about your culture?
- What facts are you most proud of regarding your culture?
- What new things did you learn about others that made you want to learn more about them?
- How was this activity a practice in listening versus just hearing? What's the difference?
- How does really listening make you a better leader? (Point out if not mentioned: To be a successful leader, you have to be engaged yourself and work to help others become engaged, as well.)
- What can you take away from this activity as you think about the fact that we will work with lots of people different from us?

TALK ABOUT PROMPTS: IT STARTS WITH ME

 20–25 minutes

 Talk About prompts
paper
writing utensils

 Make enough copies of the handout to distribute to each person.

DIRECTIONS Divide participants into groups of three. Each person has a role: one person will be the speaker; another, the listener; the third, the recorder.

The speaker in each group will choose out loud "odd" or "even," then look at the list of questions and pick an odd or even numbered question of their choice. Once they select a question, they will share a story in response. The speaker has 2 minutes to share.

The listener's job is to practice active listening by being fully present, i.e., keeping facial contact and staying focused on the speaker, really listening and not thinking about other things.

The recorder listens by jotting down any notes that piqué their curiosity about what the speaker is saying. These notes can be used for further exploring once the speaker finishes talking.

When the speaker is done speaking, then the recorder and listener can ask the speaker to "zoom in" or "zoom out" like a camera lens to either zoom in to share more details or zoom out to give context for what the speaker said. For example, the recorder might ask the speaker to "Say more about…" or "Where was this taking place?" Allow another 2 minutes for this portion.

Zooming in or out can help the speaker to think more deeply about what they are sharing.

Rotate roles so that everyone has a chance to speak, listen, and record.

Going Deeper

- Raise your hand if you feel like, if you walked away now, you would know more about yourself in a way you didn't before.
- What emotions did you experience as you went through this activity in your particular role?
- What new understanding did you gain from this activity about sharing your story? About being fully present to listen? About staying curious to learn more from the story?
- If you were to "zoom in" on a particular aspect of your own history that has really had an impact on who you are right now, what would it be?
- What would you say is a key value or belief that is really important to you as you think about the people and events that have shaped you?

Setting the Stage

Knowing our self, takes a lot of intentional work. It's the journey of a lifetime. The earlier we engage in practices that call for contemplation, awareness, and conscious choices, the more likely we will continue to engage in reflective questioning too. Self-knowledge and self-awareness set the stage for where and what we want to do next— with intentionality. Knowing our own priorities, capacities, and purpose allows us to choose how wide we want our range of influence to be. But it has to start with self, leading from within.

Talk About Prompts

If you said "odd," then pick a prompt from the odd numbers that you want to talk about. If you said "even," then choose from one of the even numbered prompts below. Choose one that appeals to you that you'd like to talk more about.

Ready? Say more about ... (pick your topic)

1. The story of my name

2. I grew up

3. I live in

4. Childhood for me

5. I look like

6. I act like my (pick a family member)

7. What I want people to know about me when they meet me

8. What is unique about me

9. A belief I hold about others

10. A value I believe we all need to embrace

11. A food important in my family life

12. My favorite way to spend my time

13. My favorite activities area

14. A dream I have for my life

15. The biggest influence in my life is

16. What I appreciate about my education

17. Something I appreciate about where I grew up

18. One thing I appreciate about my culture

19. Something that has made my life better

THE BOON

 10–15 minutes

 scenario

DIRECTIONS Read aloud the scenario and ask for responses to what each person would do in the given situation. Then discuss connecting the scenario back to values and what underlying values are reflected from the different choices.

The Boon

You're on your first away team mission and are checking out a new planet. You're getting readings on the plants and flowers when a mangy bluish grey almost catlike creature rubs against your leg. You back up quickly since you don't know what it is, but you don't leave.

It makes a mewing sound and stares at you pitifully. The animal is in bad shape and rather beaten up. It seems to be missing part of its tail. One eye is swollen and bulging out, red and weepy. The animal mews again and holds out a paw, which is bleeding with something stuck in its pads.

Your compassion kicks in and you gingerly kneel down talking soothingly to the bluish grey critter. Holding your hand out slowly, you ask if you can try to get the barb out of its pad. The creature doesn't run away, though it does stare at you intently. It seems to have even narrowed its eyes. Or maybe that was your imagination.

You explain everything as you do it, hoping to keep the unknown creature calm. Getting alcohol and bandages out of your pack, you gently swab around the wound, then yank the barb out. The creature hisses in pain and pulls its paw inward. You coo in sympathy.

Finding food in your bag, you put some out before the creature along with some water. It rubs its head against your leg. Having done what you could, you begin to take your leave. As you turn away, a voice from behind a nearby tree says, "Thank you for taking care of my num num."

You turn back startled to see a six-foot feline hovering nearby. You have no idea how she got there without you hearing her.

You gulp. Loudly. "You're welcome."

The mother asks if you are human. You say yes. She says she's heard about your kind before. She notes that you must be one of the good ones. She tells you she would like to repay your kindness and can grant you one boon. She has the ability to make you very wise, very strong, very healthy, or very influential.

Which boon do you choose? Why?

Going Deeper

- Would you help a little helpless kitten if you saw one? Why or why not?
- What about a puppy? Ask for show of hands. A bird? A turtle? A goat? A snake?
- At what point does our compassion and desire to help out someone change into a no? Why?
- What holds us back from helping others?
- What is something you're concerned about right now and would like to help make it better?
- To what person or situation would you like to magically bestow wisdom to improve a situation? What about strength? health? Being influential?
- What action can you take to broaden or deepen your concern?

THE REAL ME

 20–30 minutes

 paper
sticky notes
writing utensils

DIRECTIONS

Is This Me? (Masking the Truth)

Have each person draw their own "selfie" headshot. They can look at photos of themselves if they want. Allow 2–3 minutes to draw their self-portraits. Note that they should make the heads fairly large in size.

Next, have participants write on sticky notes and place around the outside of their face the expectations they feel others have of them: the world, parents, peers, co-workers, educators, etc. These expectations might be negative or positive but should reflect the messages they've been told or that they've heard about who they are. Give them 5 minutes to work. Check in to see if anyone needs more time and allow another 2–3 minutes if so.

Finally, they should write down on sticky notes the positive and negative expectations and messages they've said to themselves: names they've called themselves, limitations they've put on themselves, things they think they can or can't do. What do they think or say of themselves? They are to place these inside their headshots. Set the timer for up to 5 more minutes.

Tell the group that none of what they just wrote down is real. Everything they just named is part of their mask and can be peeled away just like they can peel away the sticky notes. What others think or say does not reflect their true inner self, nor do the things they say to themselves, especially the negative comments they tell themselves. The comments make up a mask of all the expectations others—and we—have set as well as the things we think might be real or what others have told us is real about ourselves.

But that's a false understanding of who our true self really is. Invite them to tear off any of the negative comments or unrealistic expectations that are holding them back and throw them away.

Y Me

Instruct the group to flip their paper over. Share that we're going to dig a little deeper to find the truth behind the mask. On the backside of the page, each person should draw out a stick figure Y (person with arms out stretched above his head) in the middle of the page.

Invite them to think about all the things they wish people saw in them and the things they really want to be true and that they see in themselves. What are the things they are that others don't see?

Instruct them to break it down. What are the qualities, dream, values you have inside you? What do you want to do? What is your reason to get up in the morning? What makes your heart sing? What are you passionate about? What is inside you already that is good and beautiful? What is it you want to do? What kind of person do you want to be? What is it the mark you want to make in the world? What are the things you want to accomplish with your life?

Write down all the things you think you truly are. (Allow 10 minutes for writing.)

Next, have them get with a partner and share their Y self and one action they can take to be more of that person instead of the person who dons the mask.

Ask for a few volunteers to say aloud some of what they learned.

Going Deeper

- Let's talk about our masks and our true selves. Why do we wear masks at times? Why do we pretend at times to be something we're not?
- Is it appropriate to ever wear masks? Why or why not?
- What benefits do we gain from wearing a mask? What does it cost us when we always keep the mask on?
- Did you write some things down that used to be true for you but aren't anymore? What were they?
- What's an example of an expectation or message you tried to meet but just couldn't keep it up?
- What's an example of an expectation or message you have rejected because you have realized it didn't fit the real you or didn't fulfill you?
- What excites you about the person you really are? What do you like about the real you?

- What prevents you from being THAT person? What gets in the way?
- What helps you stay true to your best authentic self?
- If you find your authentic self and work from there, you will be happier, more content and centered, and at the same time, help the world. What do you think of this statement? Why is being true to yourself good for the world? How does that help the world?

Conclude by having each person name one aspect of their best self that makes them proud. Prompt them to name one thing they want said about them if they can't think of something they're proud of yet. You can phrase it in the form of: Why me? Because I am _____ (fill in the blank).

BE FRUITFUL

 10–15 minutes

 writing utensil
Be Fruitful Handout
copy of Ralph Waldo Emerson quote:
To laugh often and much;
To win the respect of intelligent people and the affection
of children;
To earn the appreciation of honest critics and endure the
betrayal of false friends;
To appreciate beauty, to find the best in others;
To leave the world a bit better, whether by a healthy child, a
garden patch, or a redeemed social condition;
To know even one life has breathed easier because you
have lived.
This is to have succeeded.

 Make and print copies of this fill-in-the-blank quote by Ralph
Waldo Emerson.

DIRECTIONS Lead a discussion about any differences they see between
the descriptors "successful" and "fruitful." Which word
resonates more for them? Why? Are there other words they would use
instead that better describe how they want their lives to be? What
word best captures the idea of living a life of meaning, purpose,
contentment, and joy?

Explain that the point of the discussion is to think about the
word that most resonates with them that propels them forward in
their own growth and their own vision for the life they want to live.
Which word speaks to their imagination, creativity, commitment,
and heart? For some people, success is equated narrowly with money,
fame, or hitting an arbitrary goal that someone else set for them. But
that is not necessarily the view of everyone. Other people may find
great appeal in the word fruitful bringing to mind the image of a tree
that is rooted in nutrients, established solidly in the ground, and
able to flourish and be what it is supposed to be.

Which one of these statements most motivates you? "If you get an A on this test, you've succeeded." "If you put in the work, study, pay attention, and do your very best, you've succeeded."

Next, ask for a volunteer to read aloud the quote. Instruct the group to take this quote by Ralph Waldo Emerson, read it as many times as they want, then rewrite it for themselves. What do they want their lives to look like? What is success for them—for who they want to be or for what they want to accomplish while living in this world? How will they know their lives have been successful or fruitful? What will a life well-lived look like?

Give the group 8–10 minutes to work individually as they reflect and craft their own personal vision of a life that is meaningful to them.

When time is up, ask for volunteers to read aloud their vision for a well-lived life. Have the group do snaps or wiggle their fingers (spirit hands) after each reading. Then, if appropriate, talk about steps they each can take to live out the life they envision.

Be Fruitful

Fill in the poem to create you own guide to a fruitful, successful life.
For the last line, circle either the word succeeded or be fruitful—
whichever phrasing speaks to you more.

To _____ AND

To _____ AND

To _____ AND

To _____ , TO

To _____

To _____

This is to _____ (have succeeded/be fruitful)

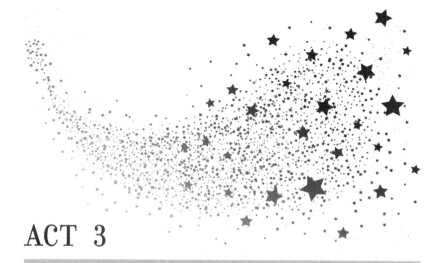

ACT 3

Leading With Others

*Look at these three words written larger than all the rest, and with
special pride never written before or since—
tall words, proudly saying "We the people.".*

*These words and the words that follow...must apply to everyone
or they mean nothing.*

—JAMES T. KIRK, "THE OMEGA GLORY"

*I am pleased to see that we have differences.
May we together become greater
than the sum of both of us.*

—SURAK

Engage

A study written by the Commission on Children at Risk, *Hardwired to Connect: The New Scientific Case for Authoritative Communities*[1], sets forth scientific findings that suggests we are biologically **hardwired to connect with each other and with meaning and purpose**. This hardwiring is in our very DNA. Think about that. Without exception each of us has a desire to give, love, and care for something more than our singular existence alone—others and some cause or core value that gives our lives meaning. You see this desire all the time in the groups you're part of. People want to belong. They crave it. They seek it out. They pursue that need to connect and maintain bonds with others. And when we act upon that deep longing, we catch little glimpses of our essential nature.

We are made for each other. We breathe in and out the same air. We share a heritage as human beings. We share the earth. We are connected in more ways than we usually acknowledge (unless we're attentively working on our leadership moves as we are as we read this book, and then we may start to pay attention).

Throw into the mix that the essence of our very nature is wired, **hardwired,** mind you, for meaning and purpose. Whew! We are indeed expressions of the Force! We are *meant* to be here to accomplish and do things that are OURS to do.

Our journey then is to find out what we're meant to do; who we're meant to be; what it is that is uniquely ours to accomplish. Armed with that knowledge, we can express our very best selves in the ways only we can because there is no one else with our exact purpose, influence, heart, talents, or desires. We are one-of-a-kind leaders gifted with an essence particular to us that only we can share with the world. We are needed to be, to lead, and to fulfill our hardwired purpose.

And.

And, along the way, we are meant to create and maintain our bonds with others, to connect in meaningful ways. At one end of the spectrum we see this through the bond we share in facing life together. At the other end, it may surface in the simple recognition

---

[1] YMCA of USA, Dartmouth Medical School, Institute for American Values. (2003). *Hardwired to Connect: The New Scientific Case for Authoritative Communities.* A Report to the Nation from the Commission on Children At Risk, Institute for American Values, 2003 (84 pages)

that we share the same breath, desires, fears, and planet. What we do and how we live impacts others. As leaders, we will have numerous opportunities to do our work in cooperation with others.

As we work together, something becomes clear very quickly if we are paying attention. We realize that everyone else is on the same voyage we are of self-discovery. We see individuals who want the same things we do. We see people who are also expressions of the Force, albeit somewhat different from us. We're all unique. And we recognize that others experience struggles, epiphanies, and adversity just as we do. Other people have doubts, qualms, quirks, talents, wisdom, dreams, and inner purpose too. They want to be comfortable in their own skin. Like us, they're trying to figure life out too. That aha moment kicks in: At our core, we truly are the same. We are indeed connected on a universal level. We are not alone. We have more in common than we ever knew. We have a shared story of humanity.

Once we begin to recognize our own power and potential to impact the common good and our innate connection with others, we realize that we can expand our influence using the Force with others. And from that base, we can enter into a reciprocal exchange of "we power" in which everyone is encouraged to give of themselves from their gifts. In this space, the connection of each person to the Force is honored and valued.

But. It takes work. We have to learn to cooperate, live, work, and lead together.

Difficult? No doubt. Doable? Absolutely. Let's look again to sci-fi to see an example of diversity in action that strengthens teams and casts a vision for what is not only possible but also achievable.

The Roddenberry Effect

Star Trek is our teacher to help us grapple with understanding what it means to truly lead well with others. When we look at the making of the television series, we see that Gene Roddenberry, the mastermind behind *Star Trek*, created a futuristic world of exploration and discovery where humanity shines brightly. His visionary work aired against the backdrop of the U.S. being in the Vietnam War and in the midst of the civil rights movement. *Star Trek* took its viewers away to new places, new encounters with other cultures, and new adventures. In the journey, *Star Trek* communicated that we (the country) can do better. We can be better.

Pause and think about what I just said was going on in the world—Civil Rights Movement, the Cold War, and Vietnam. Conflict mushroomed. Differences prevailed. Too often the story we are told is that we can't accomplish much through our differences. We need to be monotonously the same. Too many times we are pushed to take sides for either/or scenarios instead of a non-dualistic both/and approach. Competition is upheld rather than cooperation. Lines drawn. Divisions encouraged. Today, we see this increasingly taking place in everything from politics to social media streams. In recent years we have seen much on fake news versus real news and with COVID 19, to wear a mask or not to wear a mask. The term, "outrage addiction," has even been coined to describe what is happening to people whose buttons are pushed and yet continue to seek out more and more news or events that feed their anger.

I wonder if Yoda would say that Sith mind tricks are in play from the Dark Side, trying to keep everyone unsettled and at odds with each other? I can hear his voice, "Sith mind tricks, in play are."

These every day examples make it hard to believe that cooperation and living and leading well together is even possible. But it is. How do I know? Because each of us are capable of envisioning a world, a project, or a relationship better than us. Each of us desires to give our best effort to what we do. Each of us is capable of dreaming—just like Roddenberry when he put out *Star Trek* to show us his vision for the people and the world around him. His legacy demonstrated that—

Roddenberry Effect #1: **We can create a more peaceful, loving world in the future**—with commitment, empathy, listening, and work. Roddenberry modeled for all of us week in and week out inclusion and appreciation of diversity in its many forms. The crew of the *Enterprise* represented the diversity of many different groups— African American, Scottish, Asian, Russian, and even immigrants, as embodied by a Vulcan. Diversity was not a question of if. It simply was. Diversity was accepted, embraced, and a normal depiction of existence. Each individual was valued for what they brought to the ship, the mission, and the crew.

The show examined close up and personally the differences that we often face in going about our day-to-day lives: how to deal with conflicts of opinions, values, methods, beliefs, and decisions. Roddenberry brings home that unity can be achieved despite our best efforts to self-sabotage and do otherwise. The show conveys an important lesson for us to learn. The principle conduit of this lesson is from the complicated, sometimes loud, sometimes rocky friendship of three top leaders.

Roddenberry Effect #2: **Embrace diversity in all its glorious forms of expression.** Through the friendship of Captain Kirk, Dr. "Bones" McCoy, and First Officer Spock, we see three people who don't agree all the time, and two of them don't agree on much of anything. Yet they are the epitome of diversity and friendship. Bones represents the passionate emotional side of our human nature. Spock, in contrast, represents the logical side, the critical thinking aspect, of our human nature. With these natural orientations, McCoy and Spock, as can be expected, are often at odds with each other and bicker. Often. Well, at least, McCoy bickers. He is fiery and fierce, after all, and is quite vocal and emotive about a variety of subjects.

Roddenberry Effect #3: **Diversity enriches life and leads to sound decision-making for leaders good for everyone.** In spite of their disparities of approach, viewpoints, experiences, and values, Spock and McCoy are able to maintain their relationship and a mutual respect for each other, which they only grudgingly admit from time to time. And while their particular friendship keenly illustrates what opposing opinions look like and are very familiar to any of us who differ with others, these two friends move us beyond their disagreements. They model the safety they've established to be able to express conflicting points of view. They show what it is like to voice core values and still be heard. Or, in those moments when they don't listen, they demonstrate the capacity and necessity to apologize and offer forgiveness. They model leading well with others.

Of great note to us as leaders is that these two characters help balance the triad of friendship. Captain Kirk relies heavily on *both* of his officers for counsel. You see fervent emotions weighed against irrefutable logic and how both aspects come into play in making wise decisions for moving forward. Both assessments have value. McCoy and Spock illustrate beautifully in a very personal way, how people can be friends, not agree on anything, and still have stances that are both needed to see and understand the bigger picture.

Thus, by using elements gleaned from the Cold War, the Civil Rights Movement, and everyday societal tensions, Roddenbery, in a very practical way, offered his viewers alternative options for the way to move forward as a human race. At the time, Gene Roddenberry pulled off something that was revolutionary and had never been done before in television. *Star Trek* invited us all to go on a journey that could change how we engage with the world and those around us.

From this one man's vision, a television series emerged that is full of promise, possibilities, and abiding hope that humanity would discover its own humanity and realize we are more and accomplish more when we move forward together. Same humanity. Same world. Infinite possibilities. What can we do?

A Star Trek *Lesson in Action*

Here I want to highlight and expand on how *Star Trek* plays out some of its key leadership lessons regarding its mission and its commitment to seeking, out and learning from the rich diverseness that makes up our universe.

- **Continue to be open to what others have to offer. Seek out new life, new friendship, and new ideas.**

Kirk, McCoy, and Spock's friendship shows us the value of being surrounded with people who differ from us in various ways— experiences, perspectives, backgrounds, ideas, understanding, and yes, even values. When we question and push to seek to understand others as they give voice to their take on issues, we learn something. We learn something more than our singular perspective alone allows. Our perspective widens. We find pieces to a bigger picture. We discover a greater awareness of what and how life really is.

And we discover when we work together that sometimes this person is right and sometimes it's someone else. And sometimes, there's a happy medium to be found between the two. Truth often is somewhere in the middle. Kirk, McCoy, and Spock's crazy friendship points the way for us. They offer us hope.

In a world that now includes outrage addiction, if we simply seek out people who think just like us, we take the easy way out. We push differences away instead of seeking to grow and evolve in our understanding. We hold disparities at arm's length—anything that is different from us—be that people, ideas, philosophies, experiences, or politics. Anything. Anything we consider foreign to our way of doing and being is too easy to dismiss.

- **Whether it's *Star Trek*'s mission or using the Force as your guiding theme, remember the message is the same. We can all access something greater than ourselves—together.**

The way of using the Force to exert influence for the common good, nor do those actions fit the mission of the *Enterprise*. Venting and reacting are not leadership. In our Starfleet Academy training, we learn that to lead well means we accept and embrace others. When we do that, we fulfill our inborn longing to connect with others. We are actually being true to self.

Perhaps Gene Roddenberry said it best himself.

> "*Star Trek* was an attempt to say that humanity will reach maturity and wisdom on the day that it begins not just to tolerate, but take a special delight in differences in ideas and differences in life forms."

Elsewhere he reiterated,

> "If man is to survive, he will have learned to take a delight in the essential differences between men and between cultures. He will learn that differences in ideas and attitudes are a delight, part of life's exciting variety, not something to fear."

- **Never stop exploring and learning from one another and from every experience. You'll become a better leader and more influential.**

Leading well with others calls for the delight that Roddenberry describes. It requires respectful attention, a willing openness to hear others out and ask questions to understand, as well as reconsider our own viewpoints in light of other people's reality of life. We give equal weight and regard to their lives as much as our own.

Slowly, we begin to realize the truth of our universal connection. Just as we have shadow sides within us with which we must deal, so too do others. Just as we are on a journey to find out what our purpose is, so are others. Just as we work to become the best versions of ourselves—yep, you guessed it—so too are others fellow seekers of self-improvement.

In working with others, we can share our stories and take advantage of the opportunity to question, listen, and allow others to give voice to what's really important to them. And as we listen, we often learn even more about ourselves. We discover our own blind spots. We unearth our priority principles. We learn where we can flex.

- **Boldly go. Together. The future is counting on us: what we envision and what we do. We can put into action the vision Roddenberry had for a more unified, friendly world. The vision starts with us, growing together.**

It is in groups where we can express ourselves, make mistakes, change our minds, and realize what values are core to us as we slowly grow into who we really are. Members in our groups often become our teachers and serve as mirrors. In others, we see things we like about ourselves or don't like about ourselves. We know this when we have strong reactions because we love or dislike a certain quality in another person.

The beauty of leading with others is that we can sharpen each other while at the same time further develop ourselves. In teams, we learn deeper truths about our own authentic leadership and that of others. We begin to apply lessons from leading self. We put into practice self-control, reflection, and critical thinking. We enact our ability to choose how we want to respond. We start voicing and making decisions based on values important to us. We do this in concert with others who are also working to evolve.

We begin to see and own the powerful beings we are. All of us. It begins to dawn upon us that the unseeable power of the Force is everywhere and exists within everyone. Together, we can use that flow of energy to accomplish more than if we go it alone. We can expand our ripple of power into the world by getting into harmony with the members of our team. Everyone contributes. Everyone makes a difference. Everyone is needed and has a part to play.

"Make It So"

Answering the question, *Who am I?* is difficult. Equally challenging is learning to lead well with others and allowing them to be who they are without trying to make them into something else. The activities in the **Leading with Others** section offer a variety of ways for participants to develop relationships, appreciate differences, practice presence and listening, as well as grapple with their natural tendency to categorize and peg others.

As the captains of our motley crew, we want to continue to emphasize empathy, critical thinking, asking questions, and listening as instrumental components of leadership. We also want to create a safe and brave space that encourages everyone to express their opinions, values, experiences, and ideas while offering respect, humility, and willingness to learn from others. No one has everything figured out. No one has all the answers. Emphasize their interconnectedness. Name the various ways each member contributes to the group. Teach them to look for and do the same. Cultivate a deep appreciation for one another. Continue to ask, prompt, and push—especially if things get uncomfortable. Invite them to take risks. Remind them to turn to wonder when they feel judgmental or they want to cut someone else off mid-explanation. What is that person teaching them about themselves in this particular moment?

Your group will bump heads. It's up to you to show them how to navigate obstacles and difficulties to grow stronger together as a team. The activities here ask participants to explore what they know about diversity, working together, trust, and blind spots in teamwork. The processes further equip leaders to become comfortable working in teams and sharing leadership, recognizing everyone has gifts to contribute.

Don't Forget:

Consider what aids you can teach as the group begins to work together and disagree. Conflict is inevitable. Ways to handle it exist, and how to handle it is something we can teach. You can include many practices in your work to help your group gain valuable skills. I can't reiterate these skills enough as leadership tools.

Breathing, mindfulness, journaling, and meditation are all ongoing tools that leaders can tap for mastering emotions and calming inner turmoil. Additionally, these skills lead to clarity, insight, and peace of mind. These practices can result in openness and a deeper connection to one's own inner teacher (i.e. we can plug into the Force that cares for all and connects all).

Nonviolent communication (NVC) is an extremely valuable tool to handle conflict between individuals and within groups. Often, the way we speak, our body language, and facial expressions send signals as to whether or not we're really listening. Those same actions also influence the space we create for how others hear what *we* have to say and if they will even be able to hear our message.

Observations, expressing feelings and needs or values, as well as requests for actions to move forward are important steps to show true listening and a desire to keep the relationship intact while finding a way forward. (To learn more about the 4-Part NVC Process, developed by Marshall Rosenberg, PhD, read here: www. nonviolentcommunication.com/learn-nonviolent-communication/4-part-nvc/).

Role-play these skills with your team. Help the idea of nonviolent communication move from theoretical to practical. The more they are able to practice this approach, the more these steps will become a natural part of their communication process. Now that's a vision worth seeing realized! Make it so!

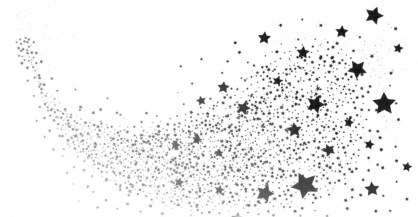

LEADING WITH OTHERS

Activities

As human beings, our job in life is to help people realize how rare and valuable each one of us really is, that each of us has something that no one else has—or ever will have—something inside that is unique to all time. It's our job to encourage each other to discover that uniqueness and to provide ways of developing its expression.

—Mr. Rogers

*We do not need magic to transform our world
We carry all the power we need inside ourselves already;
we have the power to imagine better.*

—J.K. Rowling at a Harvard graduation

DIVERSITY BINGO

 10–12 minutes

 Bingo cards (the one included here or create your own to fit a particular issue or circumstance your group is exploring) writing utensils

DIRECTIONS Distribute a Bingo card to each person. Give them 7 minutes to mingle, have conversations, and fill in as many spaces as they can on their card, only one person's signature per card. If a space indicates a choice, have them circle their pick, then sign.

Encourage them to ask questions and discover a little more beyond the topic prompter. When time is up, see who was able to fill out their whole card. Ask for volunteers to share one square from their card, the person they talked to and something they remember from their conversation.

Going Deeper

- What is something you learned about someone else that surprised you?
- What did you have in common with others?
- Where did you differ?
- What are some other categories we could ask?
- What is one way you consider yourself different from others of which you're proud? What makes you unique?
- What do you wish everyone had in common? Why?

Diversity Bingo

left handed	hair color	sweet vs. salty	country or city
bed made vs. bed unmade	cultural background	morning person vs. night owl	country vs. rock and roll
center of attention vs. behind the scenes	a people group you know very little about	pronoun preference for referring to self	doing tasks: type A personality vs. easy going
favorite way to relax	couch potato vs. busy bee	place in the family (youngest, middle, oldest)	homebody or traveler
has lived in 1 state whole life or numerous	sports vs. fine arts	favorite holiday	fine dining vs. fast food

Create Space

When we lead well with others, we keep an eye out to
make sure all voices are heard and welcomed. None
are suppressed. Value each voice. Ask people directly
if they don't speak out. Encourage others. Tell them
you want to know what they think or feel. Listen.
Create space for everyone to contribute.

DIVERSITY ICEBREAKER

 10–15 minutes

 statements

DIRECTIONS, Read aloud the statements. Have participants indicate their agreement or disagreement with each statement. (You can have them vote with their feet and move to one side of the room or the other, hold a thumbs up or thumbs down signal, etc.)

- I enjoy the Harry Potter books.
- I prefer romance novels to horror novels.
- A sense of humor is really important to me.
- I think cultural differences should be valued more than they are.
- I value my alone time.
- I like ice cream.
- I think 80's music is the best.
- Being in big groups energizes me.
- Working with my hands is important to me.
- I like to make time to be creative as often as I can.
- I think everyone should have a dog.
- I can take a stand for what I believe.
- I like playing games online.
- I like hanging out with my family.
- I like to talk by texting.

Going Deeper

- What other questions could we ask?
- How easy would it be for you to answer these questions to anyone who asks?
- Were there any questions that would take a little more time and trust for you to share your responses with others?
- What struck you about this activity?

- As a leader, you will quickly realize that no one feels the same way about everything all the time. What are the advantages of people expressing differences on the same issue? How does that help you?
- What are the disadvantages?
- How can you make sure everyone feels seen, heard, and valued even during the times when you make a decision that not everyone likes?

IN & OUT

 20–35 minutes

 whistle

DIRECTIONS, Explain that you are going to do a series of moves or tests. Participants should mirror what you call and model for them to do. They will self-assess whether or not they are successful. If they are successful, they continue to do the moves with you. If and when they are no longer successful, they call out "out!" and stop doing the moves.

Start with whistling. Next click the fingers of one hand, then switch to the other hand. Next, pat the top of your head with one hand while rubbing your stomach with the other.

Demonstrate as many nonsensical moves as you can perform yourself. You can also add in sequences such as saying, "Sally sells seashells at the seashore." 5 times in a row as fast as you can without messing up the word.

After getting several outs, stop the game.

Going Deeper

- How many of you were left out of a group at some point? Ask for a show of hands. How did that feel?
- How many of you were in a group every single time? Ask for a show of hands. How did that feel?
- What's it like in real life to be encouraged to be part of a group?
- What is it like to be left out of a group and alone?
- In what situations do you find you're chosen or not chosen?
- How do you cope with being chosen or not chosen?
- Is there a difference between fitting in and belonging? How are they different?
- As we learn to become leaders, we need to belong to ourselves first and foremost. What are some ways we can do that?

- As we lead with others, we want them to feel they belong whenever they are around us. What are ways we can be more inclusive in our homes, at school, in the community, and at work?
- When might being inclusive actually become exclusive? (Point out if not mentioned that when inclusive groups make rules of what everyone has to do to be "in," they are no longer actually inclusive. They have just put into play rules for what's in and out. As leaders, we always want to be mindful that we don't accidentally recreate the very thing we are trying to avoid!)

 Facilitator's Note

Check out this clip from Brene Brown's on sympathy versus empathy: https://www.youtube.com/watch?v=1Evwgu369Jw. Search in YouTube or at your favorite online book store to see what she has to say about fitting in versus belonging.

SELF-ID

 15–20 minutes

 scratch paper
writing utensils

DIRECTIONS, Make sure everyone has something to write on and a writing utensil. Explain that values are sometimes like a double-edged sword. There are times when your ideals put you in conflict with others, and there are times when your standards are really good for you.

Invite them to write their name in the middle and surround their name with 4 things that are most important about them. Those could be aspects of their identity like their gender, race/ethnicity, citizenship status, religion, or other important aspects about their family and where they grew up (being a Tennessean, the oldest child, or being bilingual), or even aspects of their personality like being quiet.

Give them 2 minutes to work individually and quietly. When time is up, invite everyone to find a partner. Give them 2 minutes for each one to discuss one of their items and all of its positive aspects in their lives.

When time is up, have them switch so that everyone has a new partner. This time invite them to discuss the negative aspects of one of their picks and conflicts they encounter or might happen because of that important part of their identity. Give pairs 2 more minutes to chat.

When done, discuss a little more within the big group.

Variation

Have the group break into pairs. Give them 5 minutes after completing the assessment to chat. Tell them that they cannot speak about anything related to the four things that they shared as core parts of their identity. Then, debrief what it was like to not be able to talk about the very things that are most important to them. Point out how all of us can sometimes find ourselves in situations where we don't feel comfortable being our authentic self. Reflect on what can help them be themselves more easily in all situations and what it might take.

Going Deeper

- What were some of the aspects of yourself that are really important to you?
- Why?
- How does what you value bring positivity and joy into life?
- How does what you value about yourself bring you into conflict with others?
- If we recognize that conflicts come from differing values that are important to the people in the disagreement, how can we reframe the argument so that those values are honored? (If needed, prompt more practically: For example, what do you do when one of your top principles is in competition with a value of your family?)
- How do you stay committed to what you value and also appreciate the motivating standards of others?
- Are conflicts simply a matter of right and wrong or is it more complicated than that? Why or why not?

At Our Core

We will try on many faces, values, and experiences as we slowly work towards knowing and becoming ourselves. We will at times emulate our heroes because something within them calls to us. But in the end, we have to sift through all of our experiences and influences to discern who we are at our core. By trial and error, we will discover ourselves. Be patient with yourself and never stop seeking to find your true voice.

ME TO WE

 10–20 minutes

 timer

DIRECTIONS Ask the group to mingle. On your signal, have them hold one hand up in the air and find a partner to chat with. Once they find a partner, they can lower their hands. People with hands still up in the air should look for others with their hands in the air. If it's an uneven group, create one group of three.

Ask participants to introduce themselves to each other if they haven't met. Explain that pairs will have 45–60 seconds each to talk about the topic round. You will let them know when it's time to switch.

The topic for round one is *Me,* and each person shares whatever they want about themselves. Say: What do you want people to know about you or remember about you?

When time is up, have partners stay in their same pairing. Explain that this topic round is all about *You.* One partner in each pair will start asking questions of their partner to learn more about them. Prompt: What do you really want to know? Keep track of time and let them know when to switch.

Say: When we come into groups, especially new ones, there's me and I know about me. Then there's you, and I get to know you a little bit, so now there's me and you. But the danger can now be that it's just *Us* and then all the rest are *Them*. Explain that this round is about *Them*. Invite pairs to look around and name other people here that they know and what they like about them. Give them 45 seconds total to talk.

When time is up prompt them to look around again, but this time name things they'd like to learn about others in the group to get to know them better. Ask them to pay special attention to people they don't know at all or very little. Give another 45 seconds.

Ask for a few mentions of things said about what people liked about others in the room or what they'd like to learn.

For the final round, invite pairs to join another pair so that each team has 4 people in it. Say: Our goal is to create an inclusive *Us.* Give groups 1 minute to find things that they all have in common. When time is up, ask each group, one at a time, to share a commonality. As each group reports, ask the others in the room to show by raised hand if the commonality is also true for them. Vocally note between each unifying example that includes more than the original group of four that "our ripple expands."

Wrap Up

Say: We started with me and you. We progressively moved toward creating bigger group to illustrate how we move from just *Me* and *You* to an *Us*.

You want people to get to know you and your experience. But, for people to know you, you have to do the same: experience and get to know others. The goal is to always move from *Me* to *We* to create *Us*. Same team. No *Them* versus *Us*. Just *Us*.

Our very DNA is hardwired to connect. Too often, we lose that sense of ourselves because of preferences, prejudices, or opinions. With each commonality and with each appreciation of how we're different, our ripple expands, and we become more.

Going Deeper

- What is something you learned about someone else in this activity?
- What is something you'd like to know about others in the group?
- Why do you think it's difficult to move from "me" to "we?"
- What do you think it takes to have a cohesive group?
- How have you overcome divisions in the past within groups or relationships?
- What do we need to do to make sure our group stays strong?
- What skills do we need to work on?

CIRCLE OF SKILLS

 15–20 minutes

 none

DIRECTIONS Have the group stand in a circle. Ask all to introduce themselves one at a time and name a skill they can teach others in the group or can do really well.

Direct the entire group to repeat the person's name, their skill and applaud them for what they bring to the group. Encourage people to pay attention to whom they might want to connect with or reach out to following the activity if they want to ask more questions or are curious about that person's particular skills.

Once everyone has shared their skills, provide key scenarios that are pertinent to your group and what they will be doing. Ask the group to identify which skills just named would align best with the scenario you describe. For example, if your group is going to start an online campaign to raise awareness of hunger, what skills will be needed to pull that social media campaign off?

As a facilitator, your goal is to show the group that they need more than just their own skills to advance solutions. You also want to raise their awareness that different skills are needed for different projects and challenges. Each participant in the group is needed and will have a chance to contribute and shine.

Going Deeper

Allow participants to ask for someone to say more about their expertise to further highlight the skills in the group. "You said you are good at...say more" or, "I'm really curious about..." As the facilitator, help the group probe deeper into what they know how to do and what contributed to their abilities. "What other skills or attitudes have helped you achieve that particular skill?"

The Trap

It takes awareness, courage, and discipline to resist falling into the comparison and contrast trap—to consider yourself better or worse than another person. We have to resist comparing and contrasting ourselves with others. We are no better or no worse than anyone else. Our focus is to simply develop who we are within our own unique blueprint.

ROLLING OFF THE TONGUE

 15–20 minutes

 virtual option for die: Google "dice roller" or Toytheater.com/dice/

timer

writing utensils (optional)

paper/notes feature on a phone (optional)

DIRECTIONS Tell the group that they are going to practice their presentation skills, which can be a very valuable skill for leadership. Explain that this game is a competition to see who can talk about a given topic for a set amount time, keeping the audience involved by being articulate, animated and engaging.

Go over how the activity works. You will roll the die and add 10 to the rolled number to determine the length of time for a timed chat. For example, if a 1 is rolled, the player will have 11 seconds to talk. Then you will roll the die a second time to determine how many players will participate. If a 4 is rolled, then four leaders will compete.

Ask for volunteers for the first round. Once competitors are chosen, have them leave the room.

After they leave, ask the rest of the group to pick a topic for the presenters to talk about (for example, pretend they selected bubble gum). Have the competitors come back into the room, one at a time, to talk about the selected topic for the given amount of time. Following the earlier example illustrated, all competitors would talk for 11 seconds each about bubble gum.

Once all competitors have competed, have the audience vote for the best talker by applause. Be sure to remind the group to thoughtfully applaud for everyone, but to applaud the loudest and most enthusiastically for their favorite competitor!

Repeat for another round with new competitors or do again at another session.

Acknowledge that public speaking can be easy or hard, depending on the person, the topic and/or the situation. Affirm each of the competitors by complimenting their courage, and pointing out what they did well in their timed chat. If helpful, share stories of your own public speaking experiences, what's gone well, and what you've had to work on to improve. Giving examples from your experience may help them realize that speaking is a skill that will be honed over time with practice.

 Facilitator's Note

If desired, you could have the group select a different topic for each competitor and have them all return at the same time if leaving them out of the main group is of concern. Varied topics instead of the same one may lend itself to interesting discussion points when you debrief.

You could also roll the die to identify a pre-generated topic that your group is working on or easy-to-talk-about subjects simply to practice presentation skills. Pre-selected topics could include light-hearted topics such as movies, books, vacation, healthy foods, sports, and laughter. Or, you could spark deeper thinking around leadership with topics such as diversity, peace, friendship, handling conflict, responsibility, or community concerns (fill in the blank:Hunger? Environment? Jobs? Health care? and so on). Select topics to fit the age and maturity of your group as well as your purpose.

Going Deeper

Ask the competitors:
- What struck you about this speaking experience?
- Have them finish the sentence, "I was really good at...."

Ask the whole group:

- What is a topic you have no problem talking about? Why is that topic easy for you?
- Who's ever had to do a presentation before a group of some kind? (Ask for a show of hands.)
  - What do you remember about that experience?
  - What went well?
  - What did you learn you need to work on for next time?
- Who likes public speaking? (Ask for a show of hands.)
  - What do you enjoy about speaking before others?
  - What tips would you share with those who don't like to do public presentations?
- How can you take the ease of topics you like to talk about and apply it to speaking before groups? What's one thing you could practice to make public speaking more natural?
- Why do you think leaders should work on their presentation and communications skills?

WHO ARE WE?

 15–20 minutes

 paper
writing utensils

DIRECTIONS Have participants make a list of all the different ways in which they identify themselves, the different kinds of groupings they fall under. Encourage depth, breadth, and variety. For example, someone may say left-handed, short, likes rock 'n roll music, cancer survivor, or volunteers to count birds every spring.

Give them 5 minutes to work. Ask the group to gather in the center of the room with their lists. Ask for a volunteer to name one descriptor from their list.

Have participants move to the left of the room if they can identify with that category and to the right side of the room if they can't identity with it. Have them return to the center.

Ask for another volunteer to provide another classifier. Continue asking and moving with each descriptor read.

Do as many times as desired. Aim for having every person share at least one identifier if possible.

Going Deeper

- Were you surprised at some of the different identifiers named? Which ones?
- Did you find yourself in a group at some point with people you wouldn't have guessed shared your same perspective and experience?
- What kind of descriptors did we mostly share: surface level (visible differences such as eyewear, hair color, skin color) or below the surface (one in which you have to have a conversation to really know that info about a person)?
- Which categories called out made you excited? Why?
- Of all the things you listed personally, which identifiers do you feel nail who you really are at your core or what's important to you? Name some.
- How can delving more deeply into how we self-identify strengthen our connections as human beings?

RELATIONSHIP LITERACY

 15–20 minutes

 paper/whiteboard
writing utensil
wheel of names spinner from https://wheelofnames.com/
(optional)

> **📌 Facilitator's Note**
>
> To randomize this game, use a wheel spinner with letters of the alphabet. Spin or have participants spin on their turn to see which letter they get.

 DIRECTIONS In the movie, *A Beautiful Day in the Neighborhood*, Tom Hanks plays TV show host, Fred Rogers. One particular scene shows all the crew waiting around while Mr. Rogers takes his time talking to a child. A little grumpy over being behind schedule, they nevertheless indicate this is normal. Fred puts relationships over tasks.

Mr. Rogers said, "The most important thing is that we are able to be one-to-one, you and I with each other at the moment. If we can be present to the moment with the person that we happen to be with, that's what's important." Get reactions to that statement.

Discuss within the group any times they've felt really seen or heard by someone else. What was the experience like? Who created that space? Who was present to them? Why do they remember that moment? If some participants haven't had a moment like that, what would they like an experience like that to include and feel like?

Point out that one takeaway from Mr. Rogers' example as a leader is his commitment to offer others presence. In his own words, he puts it this way: "If you could only sense how important you are to the lives of those you meet; how important you can be to the people you may never even dream of. There is something of yourself that you leave at every meeting with another person."

Invite the group to think about the impact they can have by being aware of how they engage with each person they meet. To help them do that, explain that together, the group is going to create its own relationship literacy alphabet.

Going around the group, one person at a time, each individual will contribute to the budding alphabet list by finishing the statement, "When people are with me, I..." The first person will use the letter A, the second will use the letter B, and so on until the whole alphabet is done. If someone can't think of anything within a 5-second count, they move to the end to go last, and the next person takes that letter.

Start off as the facilitator and give a couple of examples to illustrate how it works. Just be sure to emphasize which "a" word you're keeping after making the statement by repeating the "a" word.

When people are with me, I want them to feel accepted. Accepted.
When people are with me, I act nicely toward them. Act.
When people are with me, I want to allow them to be themselves. Allow.

As the group works, jot down the alphabet word for each letter. Pull out the list for the debriefing.

Going Deeper

- Which words stand out to you from our relationship literacy? Why?
- Are there other words that came to mind that you think should be included? What are they?
- Are there any words we need to change? Why or why not?
- If someone asked you how to be a good neighbor, what would you tell them?
- Where would you tell them to start from our list? What do you think is easiest to implement?
- Which particular word(s) are really important to you from this list? Why?
- Which word from our list do you want to work on being more intentional about doing so that you're expanding your relationship literacy?
- Mr. Rogers said, "There is something of yourself that you leave at every meeting with another person." If you had to choose only one idea from this list, what's the one thing you want to leave with others?

CONNECT & REFLECT

 20–40 minutes

 chart paper/whiteboard
markers
quotes

 Choose the quotes you want to use for this activity. A few possibilities are included here:

If you can't fly then run, if you can't run then walk, if you can't walk then crawl, but whatever you do you have to keep moving forward.
— Dr. Martin Luther King Jr.

The chances you take, the people you meet, the people you love, the faith that you have. That's what's going to define you.
— Denzel Washington

There are those who look at things the way they are and ask why... I dream of things that never were and ask why not. — Robert Kennedy

I am the master of my fate; I am the captain of my soul.
— William Henley

It was character that got us out of bed, commitment that moved us into action, and discipline that enabled us to follow through. — Zig Ziglar

Everything negative—pressure, challenges—is all an opportunity for me to rise. — Kobe Bryant

When they go low, we go high. — Michelle Obama

DIRECTIONS ▸ Post several quotes that have a feel of creativity and renewal and that relate to passion, purpose, and leadership. Invite participants to choose the quote that resonates most with them. Which quote speaks to them for whatever reasons?

Once everyone has made their selection, have all those who chose the same quote team up. If anyone is solo on a particular quote, they can link with a smaller group and still reference their quote. In the small clusters, invite the talk amongst themselves to explain what drew them to that particular quote. Give them 5 minutes. When time is up, ask the smaller clusters to take turns reading aloud their particular quote and reporting to the big group some of what they talked about regarding the significance of their selection.

Next, invite the group to brainstorm a list of individuals that demonstrate leadership characteristics. Challenge them to come up with 12 people with various styles and from different contexts. Chart answers. Then, using their brainstormed list, randomly choose 4 of the names and place one name in each corner of your space (4 Corners). Ask participants to select which of the 4 leaders they most connect with. Have them explain why and explore one another's perspectives. Repeat with another set of 4 leaders. Continue for 3 rounds.

When done, point out how people are drawn to others for a variety of reasons, often personal reasons based on one's values, experiences, and/or beliefs. As leaders, we have the opportunity to learn from others, especially those that we are not drawn to initially, by increasing our curiosity and openness to learning what has shaped others.

Next, invite participants to create their own leadership quote. If needed, you can prompt them with a starting statement such as "Leadership is…" or "I demonstrate leadership when I…" to get their thinking started. Collect the newly formed quotes and read them aloud. Ask the group to affirm ideas that resonate with them from each one. Invite authors to say more about their own words and their importance to keeping them focused.

 Facilitator's Note

Having young people create their own quotes is a great way to bring youth voice into the experience and it empowers participants by having them reflect on their own definitions and experiences with leadership.

Keep the quotes. You can use the quotes generated from this activity as a starting point for new groups. Sharing original quotes on leadership from past session participants adds layers of meaning, respect for youth voice, and lets current participants know that their words may also inspire those who follow them in future sessions. That knowledge can create more positive energy and greater reflection among participants.

WHO'S PEOPLE SAVVY?

 20–25 minutes

 Statements
Optional: search for free buzzer apps that can be downloaded or noise makers—1 per team

DIRECTIONS ▸ Divide the group into teams of 4–6 participants and have them sit together around a table if possible. Explain to the group that you are going to read aloud a statement. These statements cover different categories.

A team member who thinks they know the answer buzzes in (by raising their hand, rattling keys or jumping out of their seat) to say for whom the statement is true. Allow only the person who buzzes in first to answer, not the whole team. (i.e., they can't be quick to buzz then turn to their teammates to ask what they think). Watch closely for who buzzes in first.

One point is awarded for each correct answer. Keep track of points and determine the most people-savvy team in the room.

Practice round: Say aloud the Statue of Liberty or the White House. **Ask:** *For whom is it true that their city is known as The Big Apple? Name the state.* The first person to buzz in and say "New York" wins the point.

Use as many statements as desired. Mix up the categories as well. Be sure to remind the players that not all answers are one or the other—"both" might be the right answer at times.

Sample Statements are included below. Remember to repeat the answer possibilities, then ask the connected question.

Religion

Buddhism or Hinduism
   Ask: *For which religion is it true that they can worship in their houses or in the temple? (Buddhism)*

Christianity or Judaism
   Ask: *For which religion is it true that the weekly holy day is called the Sabbath? (both)*

Islam or Buddhism

> **Ask:** For which religion is it true that their place of worship is called a temple? (Islam & Judaism calls their place of worship a synagogue; Christianity calls it a church; Hinduism and Buddhism call it the temple.)

Islam or Hinduism

> **Ask:** For which religion is it true that they do not eat beef? (Hinduism. Islam does not allow the eating of pork.)

Christianity or Muslim

> **Ask:** For which religion is it true that they are the largest group? (Christianity. Muslim is the second largest religion in the world.)

Traditional Greeting Methods

Russian or Brazilian

> **Ask:** For which country is hugging warmly how people greet each other? (Russian. Brazilians shake right hands while patting the other person on the shoulder.)

Dutch/Swiss or Irish/British

> **Ask:** For which country is three pecks on alternate cheeks how people greet each other? (Dutch/Swiss)

Irish/British or French

> **Ask:** For which country is shaking hands how people greet each other? (Irish/British)

Tanzanian or Parts of South Africa

> **Ask:** For which country is spitting at each other before shaking hands how people greet each other? (Tanzania. The Maasai, a great warrior tribe, spit as a sign of blessing or good luck.)

Mozambique or Niger

> **Ask:** For which country might they clap their hands as part of their greeting? (In Mozambique, you clap hands 3 times before saying hi whereas in Zimbabwe, you clap hands after shaking hands. In Niger, you shake a fist at head level while calling out a hello.)

Romania & Ireland or France & Germany

    Ask: *For which TWO countries is "health to you" part of either their greeting or saying goodbye? (Romania & Ireland)*

Italy & Portugal or Hungary & Holland

    Ask: *For which two countries is "Good day" how they say goodbye? (Hungary & Holland. France says "good day" as their greeting.)*

Italy & Holland or Portugal & Spain

    Ask: *For which two countries is "to God" how they say goodbye? (Portugal & Spain)*

Romania or Germany

    Ask: *For which country is "see you later" a typical goodbye? (Both. Italy similarly says, "see you soon.")*

Body Language

Bulgaria or Greece

    Ask: *In which country does bobbing your head up and down not indicate "yes?" (both)*

Thailand or Japan

    Ask: *In which country does making the OK symbol with your fingers mean something different than okay? (In Japan, it means money. In France, it means worthless or nothing.)*

North America or Asia

    Ask: *In which continents is a smile used as something besides a greeting? (In Asia, people may smile when they are embarrassed. In Japan, they smile when they are confused or angry.)*

Sweden or The United States of America

    Ask: *In which country does waving your hand (palm facing outward) side to side serve as a greeting or good-bye? (U.S. In European countries like Sweden, waving the hand back and forth serves as a gesture for saying no like you're waving something off.)*

Explore More

Check out these traditions of greetings at https://247wallst.com/special-report/2018/11/20/kisses-handshakes-and-fist-bumps-how-to-say-hello-in-40-countries/print/

Going Deeper

Ask for a show by "thumb-o-meter": thumbs up for pretty savvy; wiggle the thumb if so-so; or thumbs down if not savvy at all:

- How people savvy were you when it came to knowing about different faiths/religions?
- How people savvy were you when it came to knowing about different places/cultures?
- Overall, how people savvy were you?
- What did you learn about other people?
- What similarities did you see between different people groups and cultures?
- What surprised you?
- What can you take away from this activity to equip you to be a better people person?
- What skills or attitudes does it take to connect with others?

Embrace Every

Every perspective is valued. Every person contributes. The best decisions are made when they reflect the whole, when we embrace the togetherness of us all.

DECISION TIME

 10–15 minutes

 chart paper
markers

 Write out on chart paper what each number of fingers means for reference in the activity. (Included in directions below.)

DIRECTIONS Ask the group to think about what goes into decision-making. Ask them to name examples of when they can and do make decisions alone (what they'll eat for dinner, what they'll wear…).

Ask them to name examples of when they ask others for input before making decisions (buying a car, determining a college to attend…)

Explain that when groups get together, decision-making might become easier or more difficult. Discuss and list on chart paper: What makes it easier to make good decisions in a group? What makes it more difficult to make decisions in a group?

Explain the fingers technique as a method to ensure every voice is represented when it becomes time to make a decision:

Have the group hold up one of their hands. Each finger represents an opinion. When determining their stance on choosing a service project, for example, everyone should think about their desire to pursue a given issue as well as their willingness to do so even if it's not their top issue. For example, they may not like working on water quality, but they know they have skills they can use to help in that effort.

Go over the fingers technique identifying what each finger represents, with 1 being low commitment and 5 being totally committed. Hold up the pointer finger. 1 finger is…

1. I don't like it all. Not where I want to put my time and energy.
2. I don't like it, but I will support it if that's what the team wants. I can live with it.
3. I need more information before I decide. I don't understand this well enough yet.
4. Not a perfect match for me, but I can get behind it. It's a pretty good decision.
5. I'm on board with this decision! Count me in!

In this case, when groups are putting their issue selection to a vote, they should look at where everyone is. If the majority of the group have 4–5 fingers held up, then majority vote wins. Follow suit accordingly. The group will do well to pay attention to any 3s. That will help them determine what additional information is needed (especially if the majority in the group don't have enough info—keep investigating and digging into the issues).

MY WORLD

 25–30 minutes

 statements

DIRECTIONS ▸ Explain that the group is going to explore the diversity of experiences they've had. Ask participants to vote with their feet and move to one designated side of the room if the statement is true for them or to the other if it is not true for them. Then, they'll reflect on their experience.

> ### 📌 Facilitator's Note
>
> In the list of statements below, only the first two have the complete directions (if true, go right; if not, go left). The ellipses after the following statements are a reminder to finish the voting by moving to one side or the other before turning to the debriefing questions given with each statement.

Questions are provided after each statement. You can choose to have mini-conversations and then a report from each side or ask 1–2 people to share from the different sides of the room. If time is a factor, don't ask all the questions. You can simply have them "vote with their feet" and quietly reflect.

Another experience-sharing option is to divide the group into pairs and let partners talk. This method might be best to use for any statements you feel hesitant about exploring within the big group, or if you simply want to mix methods together.

Practice round: Step to the left side of the room if you've tried any cultural type food other than what your family eats. Step the right side of the room if you have never tried a different cultural food other than what your family eats normally. Ask: What food have you tried that you now really like? What is a food you would like to try from a different culture?

Life Experience Statements

If you speak more than one language, step to the left side of the room. If you don't, step to the right.

- What is the value of knowing how to communicate in more than one way?
- Can you recall a time when speaking another language came in helpful, or you really wish you had been able to speak a different language? Who has a story?

If you have a friend who has a different cultural, racial, sexual orientation, or ethnic background than you, step to...

- How does/can having people from various backgrounds enrich your life?
- What is key to helping us reach out and get to know a variety of people of differing circumstances? What stops us from doing that?

If you have ever attended a worship service in a faith tradition other than what you're familiar with...

- What commonalities did you discover in your different traditions?
- What differences did you discover in your different traditions?
- What did you like about your experience?
- What role does faith have in uniting or dividing us?

For the next 2 statements, have the group move for each one, then debrief both of the statements together:

If you feel comfortable being in different parts of the community (i.e., are comfortable in poor neighborhoods, rich neighborhoods, on a farm, in a downtown area, etc.)...

If you feel comfortable traveling/living/visiting a different country from where you grew up...

- For both of the last two questions, around the community or around the world, where does your sense of comfort or discomfort come from in interacting with different people and different settings?

- What helps you embrace your discomfort and become more comfortable with people and settings unlike what you are used to?

If you have felt you were being treated "special" because of your gender...

- What makes gender an issue or non-issue?
- What have been the perceived positives and negatives you've experienced being your gender?
- Unfair treatment can happen because of your ethnicity, religion, financial situation, sexual identity, or even your learning differences. How can we be more proactive in making sure ALL groups, all individuals, are treated with respect and equality?

If you have friends who are older or younger than you by 10 years or so rather than just having friends who are closer to your age (under 5 years)...

- What value is there in having intergenerational relationships?
- How might different aged friends broaden your life?

If you have ever laughed, enjoyed or spent time with someone who has physical, mental, or emotional challenges...

- What impact, if any, do these challenges have on friendship?
- What benefits do you get from these particular friendships?

If you can recall a time in your life when you were with others and felt very aware of being different from the rest of the group...

- What caused your sense of being different from others? Was it a positive moment or a negative one?
- How can we maintain a positive sense of self both for ourselves and for others?

Going Deeper

- As you thought about the different experiences you've had, what did you learn?
- Is your world really diverse or not so much? How much does that assessment reflect your community and where you spend your time?
- Why is it important to think about everyone in the community when we make decisions for services offered, laws we pass, or even projects we get involved in or lead?
- Recall the very last statement asked: if you ever were aware of being different yourself in a given situation. Why do you think I asked that question?

Talk about, if not mentioned, that it is in the human condition to feel different. Feeling different is not reserved for those with learning challenges or a particular skin color or accent or gender or even living in a certain part of town or the world. We've all felt that way and not always in a good way.

Realizing that, what can we do to be more welcoming and supportive of the people we interact with each day?

BECOMING PRESENT: BE IN THE STORY

 20–30 minutes

 newspapers
news/human interest magazines
chart paper
markers

 Pre-select a story from the newspaper to use as an illustration for *presence*.

Write out questions on the chart paper:

Feel: What if YOU were one of the people in the story? What do you think brought each person to this place? What were the probable causes that led to this moment, this encounter? What are the consequences if the situation is not handled well (for each person or agency involved)?

Imagine: Was there a hero in the story? What did they do? What actions suggested awareness of presence or empathy? Where did you see signs of hope? What hopes, prayers, or positive vibes can we send to those who are involved?

Do: How could we be heroes in this story: What could we possibly speak up for? What actions could we take in light of the need we see?

DIRECTIONS Ask the group to define *presence* and *presents*. Point out that presence involves *being with*, whereas presents include *items or things*.

Ask the following:

- What is the role of presence when we engage with others?
- How does *being with* help us?

- What can we learn from being present to others, to conflicts, to community concerns?
- What helps us be more aware and present? (Say, if not brought up, that deepening our breathing and focusing on our breath is a readymade tool anyone can use to focus us in the present moment. Slowing the breath helps still the mind to pay more attention to what's going on in the now.)

Explain that the group is going to practice presence—being with—through an exercise. Start with the pre-selected story. Sum up what it's about and what it says, then discuss with the group.

What if YOU were one of the people in the story? Imagine if you were in their shoes. What do you think brought each person to this place? What were the probable causes that led to this moment, this encounter? What are the consequences if the situation is not handled well (for each person or agency involved)?

Was there a hero in the story? What did they do? What actions suggested awareness of presence or empathy? Where did you see signs of hope? What can we hope for or pray for sending positive thoughts toward those who are involved? How could we be heroes in this story? What could we possibly speak up for? What actions could we take in light of the need we see?

Divide the group into teams of 3–4. Distribute copies of newspapers to each team. (Note: Using newspapers and/or magazines provides something tangible for them to hold in their hands verses looking online.) Reveal the questions on chart paper.

Have each team look for an article and work through the listed questions. Give them 9 minutes to work, then instruct them to take 1 minute to work out what they want to share about their findings with the rest of the group. Each group will have 1–2 minutes to report.

Going Deeper

- What struck you as you applied a lens of questions to what you read instead of simply reacting to what you heard? What was different? What was the same?
- What did you value about the questions you used to guide you?
- What was different, if anything, about how you approached the news stories with the intention of *being with*?

- Were you able to practice being more present? If yes, what was that like?
- What can you take away from this exercise?
- How do you think being more present will impact your work in the community?

Vital Qualities

Grace, compassion, empathy, and acceptance are the standards we must set if we are to successfully accomplish change in the world and multiply the good we want to generate. This paradigm shift has everything to do with how we treat each other, how we engage in service, and how we advocate for policy changes. Grace, compassion, empathy, and acceptance have everything to do with the kind of world we want to create, the energy we expand, and the way we see the world. There are vital qualities that give us energy and life. They transform people and events. We must develop our own consciousness and awaken our whole selves to extend these forces to others.

PRACTICING PRESENCE

 20–30 minutes

 none

 Facilitator's Note

This activity is a follow up to Becoming Present: Be in the Story. If used as a stand alone, read through the other activity. You may want to add its conversation component on defining presence as a mini-lecture before doing this activity. The main point you want get across to the group is that you want participants to try to really see people and be present to them: WHO are they? What joys or cares do they have? This observation exercise is not a time to judge; it's a time to set aside any prejudices and assumptions. If biases arise, simply be aware of what emerges and let it go as invalid. Remind the group that their job is to seek to understand and become aware of how life is for another person and what it might be like to walk in someone else's shoes.

If going out to a public place isn't possible, consider other venues for helping your group practice presence. Can you watch together a Point of View special on PBS, or an online board or council meeting with the sound turned off and achieve the same thing?

DIRECTIONS Take your group to a public area where a variety of people are gathered (a farmers market, a food court, a public park, etc). Ask the group members to look around and simply people watch. Explain that you want them to really pay attention to people, to SEE them and think about them for a moment. What hopes might they have? What are their challenges? What might it be like to be them?

Invite the group to imagine for a few moments who the people are; what they might be doing; what their needs might be. For example, say someone chooses a nearby waitress. Imagine what her life is like. Is this the job she's going to be in the rest of her life? Is she going to school? What are the things that might limit her? What are the opportunities before her?

What about the construction worker in his 50s? What do we know about being him? What might his job be like? What does he face? Is this job a 2nd job? His 3rd? Or is it his passion?

What about the older lady cleaning in the corner? Is her job really to be a mop pusher? Is this her only source of income? Or, is she retired and this is a way for her to stay busy and connect with people? What is her life like? What are her dreams?

Invite the participants to find 1 or 2 people who catch their eye and to silently *be present with these unknown members of the community* for a few moments. As they center on different people and think of what their focus-people are doing, and what their needs and hopes are, encourage the group to really work to truly SEE these neighbors. Say: "Come beside these friendly strangers for just a few moments to be present to them. As you imagine being in another person's life, what are your hopes or prayers for that person? What do you want for them? Perhaps, you just want them to have opportunities, peace, joy, and health."

Give the group 5–10 minutes to do this activity. Instruct them to do this quietly. They can pick a place to sit and watch or walk around and observe. (If allowing them to walk, follow up with any safety rules particular to your group to make sure you keep your group together, safe and within sight of you.)

When time is up, have the group gather. Allow enough time for them to sit in silence for several breaths. Then, invite the group to bid their person of focus to be well; then in a non-public place turn to the discussion.

Going Deeper

- What was this experience like for you?
- What was it like to try to put yourself in someone else's shoes?
- Who can tell us a little about your experience and what you imagined? What came to mind?

- What did you hope for the lives of those you chose to observe? Why those particular hopes?
- How can presence—being with—and truly listening help us connect more deeply with others?
- How does the decision to be present with versus judging or assuming bring us to empathy?
- Point out that unfortunately, prejudices, judgments, and stereotypes happen. But they don't have to determine how we engage with others. We can be aware of what comes up, be wary, then choose to dismiss those influences in favor of connecting rather than letting them further separate us. What, if any, assumptions or stereotypes surfaced that you projected onto your person of observation?
- Where do those assumptions or stereotypes come from? (Point out, if not mentioned, that acknowledging the source of these things helps us disrupt our bias.)
- What other factors get in the way of us knowing other people or learning more about their lives, their hopes, and challenges?
- How does cultivating more empathy help us in our interactions with others?
- What's one important thing you want to remember about empathy and understanding that you gained from this exercise?

Add-On

Pose the question: If we could create a great town/neighborhood that includes all the people we focused on and that has all the resources everyone needs, what would that town/neighborhood look like? Then have each person take the idea of resources available to them or not available and map out their ideal town/neighborhood individually for 2–3 minutes. Form teams of 2–4 to share and expand ideas for 4–5 minutes. Finally, call for reports to the big group. You may have the opportunity to direct the discussion toward the unequal distribution of resources, pointing out the systemic injustice that is a factor in so many lives.

MEET-N-GREET

 20–40 minutes

 none

DIRECTIONS: Set up this activity by telling everyone they are going to have the opportunity to meet-n-greet and mingle with one another in the same way they would at a party. Ask them to focus on seeking out people they don't know. If they know everyone, that's okay, too, just have them look for people they don't normally talk to that much, or they can pretend they're meeting for the first time.

Give the group 5–10 minutes to "work" the room. When time is up, instruct them to pause their conversations and gather together.

Ask the group what they talked about. Get quick responses from a number of people.

 Facilitator's Note

Usually, people will say that they introduced themselves to each other, talked about their professions/jobs (school, classes, activities) and shared some personal info (like where they live, who's in their family, some of their interests/hobbies, etc.). If you want to create a visual to represent the conversations, draw a wavy "waterline" across chart paper about half way down. Then jot down a few of the quick responses on the top half of the page.

Point out that most everyone stayed at the surface by talking about "name, rank, and serial number." We have been conditioned for that kind of sharing most of our lives.

Ask: Why is that? Solicit a few responses from the group.

State: When we just focus on "name, rank and serial number," we miss an opportunity to make a real connection and find out what's most important to each of us, what really drives or motivates us, and why we do what we do, etc.

Illustrate this point by asking people to raise their hand if they know someone who has had cancer. Then, ask people to keep their hands raised if they have a close friend or family member who has had cancer. Then, ask people to keep their hands raised if they (themselves) have had cancer.

Explain that the purpose of asking for this particular information was not to garner sympathy for the people who had or have cancer, but to illustrate that with this new knowledge we have just created a much deeper connection within this room around a shared experience, something that very likely has had a profound impact on our lives.

We too often miss the opportunity to really get to know someone, even in a short period of time, when we stick with name, rank and serial number.

Ask: So, how would our lives be different, more enriched if we took advantage of our opportunities to dig deeper?

Tell everyone that they are going to mingle again, but this time their challenge is to go deeper by asking questions of one another that really *mean* something, that get at what they want to know about the other person.

Allow 5–10 minutes to mingle and then gather the group together to debrief.

 Facilitator's Note

If you chose to incorporate the waterline of visibility visual for this exercise, then ask for a few answers on the types of conversations had this time and write them below the waterline. The waterline of visibility allows you to illustrate the difference between surface-level conversations and those that run deeper.

Going Deeper

- Was this conversation harder to have? Why or why not?
- What did you talk about this time?
- What is the value of going deeper in our conversations and getting to know others?
- How connected did you feel to the other person you talked to this time around? What added to that sense of connection?
- How can we apply what we've learned here to our lives and work? To other relationships at home, in the neighborhood, or in the community?

WHAT'S IN MY HEART?

 10–15 minutes

 3–4 distinctly different heart-patterned pictures cut into 1/3rds

DIRECTIONS Distribute one heart piece per person. Give your group time to find the 2 people whose heart pieces match theirs so that collectively their pieces fit together to make a whole hearts.

Once individuals have sorted themselves into groups, explain that each group will talk about what's in their heart. Every 1–2 minutes you will signal time is up and call out a new question for the small groups to talk about.

Heart Questions

- A person in my heart who is dear to me is...
- The question in my heart right now that I want answered is...
- The thing I hear in the news that bothers my heart right now is...
- The way I spend my time that makes my heart full of joy is...
- A dream I have in my heart is to...
- The most pressing concern in my heart right now that I want to do something about is...

Say: We carry many things in our hearts: our dreams, our passions, our concerns, the people we love, and the things we love to do. Our hearts are big with possibilities. We expand our heart power when we connect with others and give and receive from our hearts. That's how we make our hearts even greater.

Invite them to talk in their groups about ways they can encourage one another and show they care.

Going Deeper

- Did any of you find you had similar heart responses or could relate to the other person? Give a few examples of your shared hearts.
- What encouraged you as you listened to each other's hearts?
- What are some of our dreams?
- What are some actions we take as a group or as individuals to begin to realize our dreams?
- What concerns were shared?
- What ideas do we have to begin to address those concerns? In particular, how can we address them from the power of our collective hearts and the passions, strengths, and dreams we share?

Wide-eyed and Childlike

If we are to move forward together as one species and one planet, we need to first work on our attitudes. We need to think about differences and conflicts in a new way. We work to cultivate the wonder and curiosity of a child as we encounter ideas, people, and experiences alien to us. Staying wide-eyed with excitement and acceptance can transform our willingness to hear others out. Being childlike helps us stay open.

THEN, NOW, NEXT

 35 minutes

 handouts
writing utensils
wall labels: 1–6, 7–12, 13–18, 19–24

DIRECTIONS▶ Tell participants that you want them to think about their early life in 6-year increments: ages 1–6, 7–12, 13–18, and finally 19–24. (Age increments are adaptable to the group you're working with. With adults, for example, you may want to do decades.)

On their papers, have them write down the different age brackets. Explain that you will ask a question and for each age category, they should think about significant influences and moments that made up that part of their lives and record their response.

- What animals did you grow up with?
- What stories were you told?
- What games did you play?
- What inventions do you remember from this time in your life?
- What foods did you eat?
- What holiday was your favorite?
- What activities did you do?
- Additional question options:
- What kind of friends did you have?
- What did you do for fun?
- What did you play with at this age?

Have participants fill out their papers for themselves: their story and memories. Give them 5 minutes to complete their papers. If desired, chart the questions somewhere where they can see them.

When individual work is done, ask everyone to go stand under the age on the wall for the most significant memory that came to mind for the animals question. Once people are gathered, give them 3 minutes to share stories.

Repeat this process for each question: choice of age for the specific question and sharing time.

For the last question, ask if anyone has an activity they want to share with the group entire group. What was the activity and how did they do it?

Variation

Have the participants chart or create a collage of their most significant memories from each age. Then have the group do a gallery walk through memory lane allowing each person to share a story or two from their particular chart.

Going Deeper

- You've talked about life experiences that meant something to you. As you think about the different things that were important, what do you want to keep as you move forward into the next six years? Do you want to play more? Read more? Be intentional with how you celebrate or integrate old traditions into new? What?
- What else do you think might become important to you in the next six years?

The Force Within

Each of us has to distinguish the differences in the Force within us. What is me at my best? What is my work to do? Where is my voice? What is it I think and believe? What is mine to express?

MARKED TIME REFLECTION

 10 minutes

 markers (or pens)

DIRECTIONS, Divide the group into small teams of 4–8 and have them sit in a circle. Hand the marker to one person in each group to start.

Someone else in the group will pick a question to ask that person about the topic from the session or the time together. For example, what are five things you learned today? What are four games you want to remember from today? What is the best idea you heard from someone else? What are two ways you are going to implement what you learned into your service project? What are four ideas you are excited about trying?

After the question is asked, the person holding the object passes the marker to the person next to them and begins answering the question as the group passes the marker from participant to participant. Once the marker comes back to the one answering the question, that person can stop talking. Emphasize that only the person who starts the passing of the marker can talk after the question has been asked. Everyone else listens as they mark the time by passing the object along.

Repeat process: The participant holding the marker gives it to someone new. Another reflection question is posed from the group and the object passed to mark the time as the answerer proceeds.

Going Deeper

Ask within the big group for volunteers to share something from within their small group discussion that caught their attention or was interesting to them.

WALLETS, POCKETS, AND PHONES

 5–15 minutes

 supplied by participants

DIRECTIONS Divide the group into small teams of 3–5 participants.
Explain that for every letter of the alphabet, they are to
gather an item, one item per letter (such as D for dime and P for
phone, etc.), and bring them to the facilitator. The team that brings
up as many items as they can find that fits as many letters as possible
within 10 minutes wins the game.

The rules are this. Each team will bring up their items, one at a
time, in alphabetical order to show the facilitator. All gathered items
should come from what the participants have with them: backpacks,
purses, wallets, etc.

 Facilitator's Note

Normally the people who bring the items up to
show what they have are the ones who own that
item so returning things to their proper place is not
an issue. However, if you expand the resources to
include things found in your space or if your group
just needs to hear it, remind them to return all items
to where they found them. They should pay attention
and remember where they got things from.

Variation

Instead of covering the alphabet, run quicker rounds of 1 minute
each for teams to gather as many items as they can that fit a
particular letter (for example, P might have a penny, phone, photo,
pencil, purse, pocket, etc.).

Going Deeper

- How did your team work together?
- How did you communicate?
- How would you have done if you had played this solo versus having partners? How successful would you have been?
- Why is working with others important? What do we gain from pooling our resources, both material and as individuals?

FILL IT UP!

 5–15 minutes

 4 same sized empty bottles
4 sponges
4 containers of water
masking tape (the blue kind is easier to peel up)

 Fill containers with water and place equidistance in 4 spots along the starting line. Place a dry sponge next to each container.

DIRECTIONS, Play this game in a space that is easy to clean up afterwards. Divide the group into 4 teams. Line each team in parallel lines, with approximately 10 feet between each teammate. Give each player 2 small pieces of tape to make an X on the floor. Have them stand on that spot. Distribute an empty water bottle to the person at the finishing end of each line. At the start of the line is the bucket, sponge, and first player from each team.

When you say "go," the first person in each line dips their sponge into the water soaking it thoroughly, then they toss it to the next person in line. The sponge is passed from person to person to the last player who squeezes as much water as they can into the empty water bottle. Then, when they are satisfied that they've gotten as much water into the bottle as they can, they then run to the start of the line to re-soak the sponge while everyone on their team moves to the next taped X spot on the floor.

The sponge is then tossed again down the line to the last person who tries to squeeze as much water as they can into the empty water bottle. Rinse and repeat (ha!) until everyone is back in their original starting place.

Ask for any clarifying questions, then tell the teams to go.

Compare the bottles when done. The team with the most water in their bottle is named the water champions.

Going Deeper

- What did you like most about this task?
- What was most difficult?
- When you heard what the task was, did you think you would be able to achieve it? Why or why not?
- What would you do differently next time?
- How important was being careful to this activity?
- Did competition cause you to get sloppy instead of doing the task well?
- How can being competitive get in the way of our work as a group?
- What are some challenges our community faces that feel difficult or impossible?
- Why is it important to try even if the odds feel stacked against us?
- What is something you've invested in that didn't pan out the way you hoped but it was worth the effort?

THE BEST

 5–15 minutes

 2 sheets of scrap paper

DIRECTIONS ▸ Divide the group into teams of 3–4. State that everyone has to participate in at least one round. Cover the rules: A contest category will be announced, such as The Tallest, and each team must select one person who they think will win the category. If a person has the best in the given category, they win admiration of all for their team.

Give them all the different categories you've selected. Let them decide who will take each one. For each category, have appointed team members come up. Then reveal the Real Measure and determine which of the participants wins the round. Repeat. Be creative in your connections between the category and the actual measurement. Have fun with this.

Stated Categories—Real Measure

- The Tallest—thumb
- The Shortest—eyebrow length
- The Most Flexible—shoe
- Smiley—whose face crinkles the most with a smile
- The Brightest—whose hair is the lightest in color or brightest shine
- The Bounciest—can juggle 2 paper wads
- The Most Petite—freckle on the back of your hand

Going Deeper

- What surprised you about this game?
- How did you react to finding out what you thought and what was real differed?
- How long did it take you to recover and go with what was happening?

- When we expand our circle of friends and coworkers, we often encounter surprises, different perspectives of same experiences, or different experiences altogether. How do you want to respond when you encounter people and events that are different than you think?
- Why is being open an important part of relationships?
- How can you cultivate and keep a sense of humor, like in this game, when things turn out differently from your expectations?
- What else did you learn from this activity?

NAME THE NAMES

 5–12 minutes

 writing utensils
paper
timer

DIRECTIONS Divide the group into teams of 3–4. Provide each team with a writing utensil and paper. Explain that you will announce a letter of the alphabet and either male or female. Each team needs to list as many names that start with the letter and the given gender as they can within 2 minutes. Announce a random letter and gender.

After 2 minutes, have the first team read their entire list aloud. If any other teams had written down any names that are called, they should cross those names out.

Continue until each team has reported.

Going Deeper

- Were there any names that were new to you? What were they?
- How many of you only thought of names from your own culture?
- Did any of you think of names outside of your culture?
- What primary cultures did our list of names reflect?
- How long of a list do you think you could have made if you had tapped even more cultures?
- Did any of you create new names? Or did you tap some of the methods you see online for making your Klingon name or your rapper name, for example?
- Learning names, knowing them, pronouncing them correctly, and using them is a first step in getting to know someone else and showing that you see them and care. What's another step in developing good relationships with other people?
- What's an action step you can take to diversify your world just a little more?

TWO BY FOUR

 10–20 minutes

 paper/whiteboard
writing utensils
timer
die
virtual option for die: Google "dice roller" or go to Toy Theater
(https://toytheater.com/dice/)

DIRECTIONS Instruct the group to get into pairs. Explain that you are going to roll the die and announces the number. The pairs will seek to find that many things they have in common in 40 seconds and jot them down. For example, when a 3 is rolled, Jacinta and Lamont discover they both like pizza, or they both play soccer, or both of them have a middle name that starts with a "G."

Ask for any questions. Set a timer for 40 seconds and tell them to go!

When time is up, have pairs join up with another pair to create teams of four. Again, roll the die and announces the number rolled. During the next 40 seconds, the newly formed quartets seek to find the new target number of things that all four of them have in common.

When this round ends, give quartets 40 seconds or less to determine the most interesting thing they have in common, something that they think others in the group won't have on their list. Go around from team to team and have each one announce their interesting commonality.

As facts are reported, ask the rest of the group if anyone else also relates to the statement read.

Going Deeper

- What struck you about working to create your lists?
- What methods helped you quickly find things you had in common?
- What changed in moving from two people to four people? What was that round like?

- Were you surprised by the number of things that people in our group have in common?
- What else would you like to see if anyone else has in common with you? (Allow participants to name items and ask for a show of hands if anyone shares that commonality.)
- How does finding connections with others affect relationships?
- Why, do you think, as a leader it is important to seek common ground?
- How can finding commonality in a group help move ideas, projects, or change forward?

Sorting

Unfortunately, we will be exposed to conflicting messages and voices every day. We will have to sort through the various influences to determine what is true, right, beautiful, and good

CHAIN OF LIFE

 20–30 minutes

 strips of paper
pairs of scissors
staplers

 Select the statements you'll be using and write them individually on strips of paper. Ensure each person in your group has a stapler, a pair of scissors, and enough strips of paper to match the number of statements you'll make, especially if you decide to do this activity virtually.

DIRECTIONS ▸ Explain that the group is going to make paper chain links to reflect their life experiences to date. To start, you will call out an incident, then hold up the slip of paper with that event on it to show the group. They should write down the key idea from what you read onto a strip of paper, and then they will either star the statement or make a tear in the chain depending on the directions of the statement. Finally, they will staple the ends of the paper together into a circle.

Do a couple of statements together as a demo such as make a star if you have had 8 glasses of water today. Instruct them to record the key word, star or tear, and then staple the ends together. Do another example such as make a little tear in your chain if you haven't exercised today. Again, have them record the key word, tear or star, then have them slip the paper through the other link and staple the ends.

Working through two links will make sure everyone gets into the rhythm of writing, starring or tearing, linking, and stapling. After you've completed the demonstration start the activity. Remind them that the process is to write, cut or star, link and staple. Repeat.

Make clear that experiential statements are not a finite list of life opportunities. This activity is simply one snapshot of what persons may have experienced to this point so that the group can have a discussion. To that end you can say something like: "This activity will let us see the variety of starting places we have in life along with the different impacts and influences we've experienced."

Perspective Statements

- Make a little tear in your chain if you made a mistake this week. (For example, the key word may be "mistake.")
- Make a little tear in your chain if one of your parents has been unemployed or laid-off, not by choice.
- Star the keyword on your chain if you have attended a private school for classes or camp.
- Make a little tear in your chain if your family ever had to move because they could not afford the rent.
- Make a little tear in your chain if you were ever discouraged from particular classes or jobs because of religious beliefs, race, class, ethnicity, gender, or sexual orientation.
- Star the keyword on your chain if you were encouraged to attend college by your parents.
- Make a little tear in your chain if you have ever felt you were being treated unfairly because of the shape or size of your body or a physical blemish of some kind.
- Star the keyword on your chain if your family owned the house where you grew up.
- Star the keyword on your chain if you have ever been offered a good job because of your association with a friend or family member.
- Make a little tear in your chain if you have ever been denied employment because of your race, ethnicity, gender, or sexual orientation.
- Star the keyword on your chain if you feel you were treated fairly because of religious beliefs, race, ethnicity, gender, or sexual orientation.
- Make a little tear in your chain if you have ever been accused of cheating or lying because of your race, ethnicity, gender, or sexual orientation.
- Star the keyword on your chain if your family ever inherited property.
- Star the keyword on your chain if you have ever gone out of your way to get to know someone different from you (race, ethnicity, gender, or sexual orientation).
- Star the keyword on your chain if you speak more than one language.

- Star the keyword on your chain if your family has a saving account.
- Make a little tear in your chain if you have ever been stopped and question by the police because of your race, ethnicity, gender, or sexual orientation.
- Make a little tear in your chain if you have ever been afraid of violence because of your race, ethnicity, gender, or sexual orientation.
- Make a little tear in your chain if you have ever been uncomfortable about a joke related to your race, ethnicity, gender, or sexual orientation but felt unsafe to confront the situation.
- Make a little tear in your chain if your parents did not grow up in the United States.
- Star the keyword on your chain if your parents told you could be anything you wanted to be.
- Star the keyword on your chain if your parents held professional careers like doctors, lawyers, teachers, or professors.
- Make a little tear in your chain if you've ever tried to change something about yourself (appearance, the way you talk, or how you act) to avoid being made fun of or judged in some way.
- Star the keyword on your chain if you see people of your race widely represented in a job you think would like.
- Star the keyword on your chain if you or your family vote.
- Make a little tear in your chain if you've ever felt isolated or left out by others in some way.
- Star the keyword on your chain if you agree with this quote from Alice Hoffman: *My theory is that everyone at one time or another has been at the fringe of society in some way: an outcast in high school, a stranger in a foreign country, the best at something, the worst at something, the one who's different. Being an outsider is the one thing we all have in common.*

Have everyone hold up their links. Remind them that this moment is only a snapshot of what they've experienced so far. And it is a moment of invitation to reflect on the kind of life they want to have, the people they want to have in their lives, and the experiences they want to build in to better equip them as leaders. Emphasize that while not everyone has had the same advantages, opportunities, experiences, or backgrounds, this activity simply shows a little bit about what life has been to this point. Some people have experienced rough patches; some individuals have lived sheltered lives; others have had greater advantages than most. None of what has happened speaks to their abilities, gifts, decisions, strengths, or resiliency. Nor is their past a reflection of who they are.

Going Deeper

- What's your reaction to the quote (above)?
- Does the quote give you comfort as you look at your own chain link?
- Instruct the group to look back at the keywords and how they rated them.
- In what ways have our past experiences shaped us positively?
- In what ways have our past experiences added hurdles to our day-to-day lives?
- What about right now? What's going on in life right now that might be hindering or helping you?
- If you had fewer than you want, how can you cope? What connections do you have that help you face life's challenges?
- Which links do you want to change or get rid of?
- What's your plan to make change in that area? What action steps can you take?
- What experiences on your links do you want to build on?
- What steps can you take to strengthen those areas?
- How important is it to hang on to a support system?
- How can we learn from the variety of experiences we've had to be better leaders and friends?

Wrap Up

Invite them to hang up their links where they can see them. Challenge them to add to their links this month. Point out that as leaders, each of them has the ability to influence their own lives in some way, be it small or big. How can they enhance their own lives to attract the experiences, people, and attitudes that enrich their lives?

Without Fear

Leading well means creating a space where everyone belongs rather than just "fits in." All can show up and express themselves bravely and safely without fear of rejection.

SNAP!

 15–20 minutes

 flash card set of words (optional)
paper
writing utensils
chart paper/whiteboard
marker

DIRECTIONS Explain to the group that they are going to do some word associations. You will show them or say a word or phrase, and they have 15 seconds to write down the first thing that comes to mind. No judgments. There is no right or wrong answer. This is simply what bubbles up first.

Ask them to number each response as they go. Do an example together out loud. Give the phrase "peanut butter" and ask for a couple of people to say the first word that popped into their heads.

After going through your numbered list or set of cards, select a few you want to spend more time with and list those on the left side of chart paper. On the right side, as a heading, put a plus sign, a zero (for neutral), and a negative sign. Draw lines down between each sign to make columns. Ask for a show of hands of those who had a positive reaction to the first word. Be sure to remind them what number it is. Then ask for a show of hands for a neutral response and negative response, respectively. Record the number of responses in the appropriate column by the word.

Repeat this process for each of the charted word, then discuss.

Sample Word Set

trailer-park residents
red necks
athletes
southerners
rich people
mentally ill people
Muslims
transgenders

homosexuals
geeks
Buddhists
teen moms
Christians
red heads
politicians
Asians

lawyers	taxi drivers
farmers	poor people
brunettes	Caucasians
prisoners	poor people
visually impaired people	postal workers
school administrators	custodial/janitorial staff
blondes	servers
bad tippers	teen dads
teachers	physically challenged people
the elderly	teenagers

Going Deeper

- As a group, did we have more positive, neutral, or negative reactions as a whole? Why do you think that is?

- Where do you think some of the negative responses come from? What about the positive ones? What influences those different reactions?

- We made off-the-hip responses to the words. We often make instantaneous, snap reactions to other people that tend to impact our behavior towards others because sometimes we judge others without knowing anything about them. Why do we do that?

- Where do you think those instant categorizations come from?

- What factors contribute to stereotyping and pre-judging?

- What are the consequences of labeling? How does typecasting impact the person/situation you evaluate? How do snap judgments impact you and how you behave?

- How can we curb our seemingly natural tendency to make a snap critique of a situation or someone else before we really know what's what or know the person better?

- Once we learn to recognize what we're doing, what deliberate actions can we take to move forward thoughtfully with attentive awareness?

- What does it take to be someone who keeps an open mind and is respectful of all people?

- How does asking questions help us challenge things we've assumed?

- What is one thing you'll take from this activity?

DEFINE YOUR VISION

 15–20 minutes

 paper
writing utensils

DIRECTIONS Invite your group to draw two stick figures on a sheet of paper drawing one on the far left side and the other on the far right side of the page. (You may want to draw out an example as a visual on chart paper/whiteboard.)

Instruct them to label the word "present" above the stick figure on the left. Around that figure, ask them to write down 3–4 words of how they would describe themselves today. What are their core characteristics, strengths, challenges, etc.? Give them 1–2 minutes.

Next, have them label the stick figure on the right as "future" self. Who's the person they want to become? How do they see themselves as their very best? What qualities do they want to expand? For example, what strengths do they want/need to develop to overcome challenges? What values do they want to deepen? What character traits do they want to keep at the forefront? What do they want to accomplish? Have them write down 3–4 words around their future self that reflect their answers to those questions. Give them 3 minutes.

Instruct them to draw 3 stacked arrows between the two figures, leaving plenty of space (think 5 sentence paragraph width) between each of the arrows so they can write down ideas on top of each arrow. The arrows point from their present reality to their future self to indicate forward motion toward their vision. Instruct them to label the top arrow to one side as "start," then identify one action that they can begin today that moves them closer to their vision of who they want to be and what they want to accomplish. What moves them closer to their vision of who they want to be? Give them a minute to work.

Next, after labeling the middle arrow "continue," they should identify one action that they will keep doing because it is aligned with moving them toward their vision. What will they continue to do because it aligns with their vision? Give them a minute to work.

Finally, the bottom arrow should be labeled "stop." Here, each one names one action they should quit doing today that will aid them in achieving their goal of becoming the best version of themselves possible. This action should indicate something that no longer serves them well and gets in the way of them growing and becoming. The item they discard might even be a habit or an attitude. What will they stop doing because it holds them back from being their truest self? Give them a minute to work.

When the group is done, ask everyone to find a partner. Give time for each partner to talk about 1 action step they will take this week to keep their vision moving in the direction they desire and want to create. Allow 2–3 minutes.

Invite group members to hang their vision somewhere at home to serve as a visual, daily reminder of the person they are aspiring to be, what they want to achieve, and the tangible action steps they are going to take to make it come true.

Going Deeper

- What excites you about the person and leader you envision?
- What steps are easiest for you to take?
- Why is it important to pause and reflect on who we are and where we are?
- What role do you think actually inking down your vision has on your ability to carry out your vision?
- What will help you reach your personal vision?
- Who can you lean on to support you as you seek to make changes?
- What will help you stay on track to work the steps and move forward? What do you need to put into place to hold yourself accountable?

LOST IN _____

 15–20 minutes

 writing utensils
paper

DIRECTIONS Divide the group into 2 or more teams of 4–8 participants each. Ask each team to identify where they would like to be lost or stranded if they had to be: The moon? In space? Mars? On a deserted island? After the teams have named their adventure, Lost In _____, say more about the scenario. Everyone is lost and stranded (fill in the blank for each team). The situation is grim. Help may not arrive for months or years. Each participant should think about the one object they would bring with them or make sure they have and why. Ideally, the object would represent them or something that they enjoy. Give 1 minute for quiet reflection and perhaps jotting down of notes.

 Facilitator's Note

The objects brought don't have to be survival oriented. Rather, encourage them to bring things that truly express who they are or their interests. For example, if someone loves football, they might bring one. A cat lover might bring a cat. A coffee lover might bring a can of coffee. A lover of music might choose to bring a radio. Encourage people to choose something that is special to them.

After they've had time to think about what they'd each bring, announce that each team has 10 minutes to discuss and brainstorm. First, each member should describe what they brought and why. Then, after everyone has spoken, they are to work together to improve their survival chances by considering how they might combine or use their objects together. Every item must be used as they establish their new life.

As you listen to the different discussions, you can, as facilitator, randomly add in more objects that fit their storyline. Perhaps an oar floats ashore or they find in the wreckage of their ship on Mars dry rations.

When time is up, give them 2 more minutes to prepare what they will report to the others about their new life situation: their items and how they're using them to survive. Have each team speak and allow time for others to ask questions after each report.

Going Deeper

- What did your learn about your teammates?
- How well did you work together?
- What was one of the most interesting ways you found to meet your challenge for survival?
- How does necessity spark creativity and inventiveness?
- What did our choices say about what we value as a whole?
- Did we lean toward the arts, cultural heritage, personal hobbies, or something else?
- Why do you think the emphasis was on what we value and expression of who we are versus going straight for basic components to survive?
- How important to your everyday life are the things you chose? Why or why not?
- What makes up a good quality life? What do you need to have?
- Research talks about life aspects that help us thrive—things like interests, passions, and purpose—like some of the items you named. How can we ensure everyone has what they need not just to survive but thrive?

ULTIMATE TEAM MEMBER

 40–60 minutes

 chart paper
markers
tape
sticky notes
pens

DIRECTIONS Divide the group into teams of up to 15. Explain that they will create their ultimate team member. First, instruct them to create the outline of a person. They can have someone lie down on paper and trace their body on the chart paper or simply create a big drawing of a person.

Invite everyone to individually consider what they could give to a team that was trying to accomplish something? Instruct them to reflect quietly and write down 3 or more characteristics, qualities, or skills they possess. Give them 2 minutes to work.

Then, as a team, they should think collectively and each participants say aloud 3 beliefs of inner strengths (characteristics) they think an ultimate team member should have. The group should record all answers on sticky notes, one per sticky, then post their ideas inside the outline of their person. Give them 8 minutes to work.

Once the discussion is done, have each team name their ultimate team member. Then, ask groups to write a front-page story of this person. What do they do? How do they act? How are they in the world? How do they engage with the world and others? How do they change the world or others? How do they make it better? What makes them the ultimate team member when they are in this group's space for an entire day? How do you see it and know it? Give them 12 minutes to work.

When time is up, tell teams they will have up to 5 minutes to present their ultimate team player to the others. They will present their person by introducing their character by name and reading their story. Someone from the presenting team will pull off a characteristic or skill one-by-one as it is named aloud.

Meanwhile, as the story is being read, anyone in the whole group who feels they have that skill should step forward boldly to be seen and to own their skills and strengths with pride. Have the rest of the group do fingers snaps as people step forward.

Continue until all stories have been read and all skills applauded.

Wrap Up

How beautiful it is to tell the story of a group working together as one unit within in a space whether that space is at home, at school, at work, in the neighborhood, or the community.

I've already met these people (call out the different names created by each team). I've met them because I've met each of you. By working together, you collectively become the ultimate team and can accomplish so much.

Going Deeper

- Now that you've named some of the strengths and skills you have individually, how can your strengths help you through challenges?
- How can you apply them to make your life better?
- How can you tap the power of your collective strengths to do something incredible? What project could you do? What issue could you tackle to improve it?
- Do you think you might be more successful in planning activities utilizing the strengths identified in your "ultimate team members" as opposed to doing something alone? Why or why not?

Together

Working well with others brings deep satisfaction. Learning to lead with others diminishes fear, helplessness, and hopelessness. Together, as change makers, we can shape the future in the direction we desire.

HUMAN CREATIONS

 35–40 minutes

 YouTube clips and way to show them (optional)

DIRECTIONS ▸ Ask for a show of hands of those who've seen the movie, *Hugo*. Explain that Hugo Cabret lives behind a clock. He is fascinated with building and fixing machines. He knows that machines don't come with extra parts and that every part has a purpose.

Divide the group into teams of 4–6. Invite each group to craft their own human machine. Allow 12 minutes to plot out what their machine will be. As Hugo said, there are no extra parts. Everyone has a reason and a role in the machine. Make and use all the parts!

Remind them to honor safety first as they figure out what they will do. And, they must create an ad or jingle for their machine.

When time is up, ask for each group to demonstrate their machine.

The Game in Action

At one retreat, my group was given a toaster to create. Four people stood in two lines, two to each line, while one person—the toast— squatted between them, and the final person operated the button to turn the toaster on. They sang a jingle to the tune of I'm a Little Teapot that went like this:

"I'm a little toaster. Here's my slot. Put in the bread and make it hot."

The bread popped up when the group shouted out, "Pop! Toast is ready!"

Going Deeper

- What do you think about that idea that your life really and truly matters to the bigger picture?

- What do you know about your reason to be here, your purpose? Specifically, what do you think is your purpose right now?
- If you can't name it yet, do you have any clues as to what it may be?
- The things you love to do, your favorite activities, the skills you like using and are good at using are all clues to identifying your sparks—that fire within you that brings you joy and energy—a precursor to purpose. What do you like to do and are good at doing?
- Can you name a time you used your skills, knowledge, or talents in a way that felt energizing, satisfying, or joyful that made a difference to someone else? Ask for a few examples of what they were doing and why it mattered.
- The movie points out that we all had different ways to contribute and that we couldn't do it all by ourselves—each part is needed—and we're more successful when we work together. What has been your experience of being more successful when everyone contributes and pulls their weight? Can you think of an example to share from home, in school, on a team, in the community, or in this group?

Add-Ons

If you want to extend the conversation, this clip from the movie or quote provides the opportunity to talk about when things are broken and don't work well:

- Video (1 minute 36 seconds)
  http://www.youtube.com/watch?v=kPYWFyDdYno
- "Maybe that's why a broken machine always makes me a little sad, because it isn't able to do what it was meant to do... maybe it's the same with people. If you lose your purpose... it's like you're broken."—Hugo

Going Deeper

- What do you think of Hugo's observation?
- What is a usual response when a team hits a wall and seems "broken?" What tears a group down? Why?

- What ideas do you have for when our team tears down? How can we not let obstacles "break" us?
- Do you think that if we keep our purpose front and center, utmost in our attention, that it would help us stay more focused and work well together? Why or why not?

 Facilitator's Note

If you are in a phase of planning a service or advocacy project, you might want to follow up the activity with brainstorming the barriers the group is facing in trying to help the community, and then go into a planning stage for how to address the various obstacles. Use the What? So what? Now what? reflection technique:

What obstacles are we facing?

So what does it mean? (to our project, to the issue, to our vision? Will these obstacles derail us from doing this project, working with this resource, redirect where our efforts need to be spent...?)

Now what can we do? (Identify what your group can do and what action steps you will take to overcome the obstacles and continue on with your efforts.)

Set goals for self-actualizing success as your group identifies their action plan.

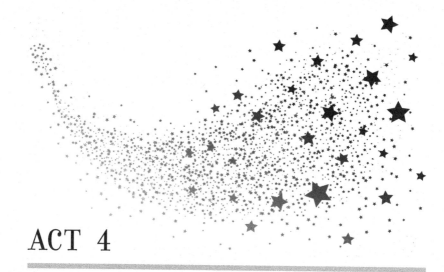

ACT 4

Leading in a Digital World

Young people should be at the forefront of global change and innovation. Empowered, they can be key agents for development and peace. If, however, they are left on society's margins, all of us will be impoverished. Let us ensure that all young people have every opportunity to participate fully in the lives of their societies.

—KOFI ANNAN

It is from numberless diverse acts of courage and belief that human history is shaped. Each time a man stands up for an ideal, or acts to improve the lot of others, or strikes out against injustice, he sends forth a tiny ripple of hope, and crossing each other from a million different centers of energy and daring, those ripples build a current that can sweep down the mightiest walls of oppression and resistance.

—ROBERT F. KENNEDY, SOUTH AFRICA, 1966

Digital Group Guidelines

Two things are needed, for sure, to maximize the potential of an online environment: engagement guidelines and techniques to keep the interactions real and active.

Whether you are a teacher or leader of a small group of folks (youth or adult) or leading online workshops for professional development, you still have to create the space. Here are a few engagement guidelines that I, and other practitioners, find effective. Peruse the list and see what works for you.

Online Meetings and Trainings Best Practices

Ready your group tech wise. Send out a notice or practice with your group so they are comfortable getting onto your online platform, and you don't have to waste time during the actual meeting/training to cover the how-to's of using technology. For example, with Zoom, before your meeting, send out an email or video that reminds them to—

- Download the Zoom app, if needed.
- Add their name and, if desired, their picture to the profile (profile pictures show when video cameras are turned off).
- Log in a couple of minutes early to make sure the tech works smoothly.
- Contact you if they want a quick practice session with you coaching them on how to use the tool. (Some people learn best with a walk-through.)

Encourage presence and being present. In a face-to-face group, it's easier to quickly tell when someone wants to talk. Online, participants can raise their hands (literally or using the nonverbal tools available online) to say something.

- Do ask people to have their video on when they join.
- Ask them to look directly at the camera—simulating looking directly at others. (Yes, it feels counterintuitive, but remind them of the listening skills they would use if they were in an in-person conversation.)
- Courtesy practices suggest having the audio muted as they join. (Both video and audio settings can be set as default on

the participants' end.) Encourage participants to speak, but you may need to remind them to unmute themselves when they want to enter the conversation. Also, ask them to mute themselves when not talking in order to block distracting background noise.

Set bio and screen-free breaks. Set frequent breaks during longer meeting/training times—at least every 1½–2 hours. Our biological bodies need to expend energy and recover. Have the group get up and walk away from the screen for 5–8 minutes (walk, get water, take care of physical needs, look outside or anything not a screen).

Set a limit on the size of your training. Engagement online can be a little tougher than face-to-face, so set a limit for the number of people you feel you can comfortably engage in your training event to maximize involvement and learning.

Have a co-host. I have always been a fan of 2 trainers for groups of 15 or more. While one is teaching, the other can read the group and answer questions on the side. Online training makes having a buddy even more important. Your co-host can work the mechanics required of Zoom and other online platforms (putting people into breakout rooms, looking for questions in the chat feature, and so on) while you pay attention to the content and leading the activity.

Create a participant-friendly environment. We know that it's important to use names, be respectful, and include everyone. Online, there are some little tweaks we're all learning, such as—

- Asking people to give full attention to the meeting/training when it's happening. Thus, they need to be on camera the whole time. We want to see their faces. However, no walking around or rocking in a chair. While understandable, it can make others dizzy watching!
- Asking people to remember to dress appropriately. Be professional. Did we ever think we'd have to remind people to wear pants or be aware of the V-neck shirt when they lean forward? (My favorite meme said absolutely no *Star Wars* apparel shall be mixed with *Star Trek* clothing!)

Protect the group. Get your training participants to R.S.V.P. so that you have their emails and know who is supposed to show up to your training. When I run a training on Zoom, I activate the waiting room so that they go there, and I see who is in the waiting room. I can then admit those I know are supposed to be coming or names I recognize (in case they forgot to R.S.V.P.) When all participants are in, I can then lock the meeting (or lock it after the first 10 minutes are up) to secure the group from people who aren't supposed to be there. If you do decide to lock a meeting after a set time, let your participants know ahead of time that that's going to be your policy in order to keep the group safe.

Facilitators, Be Aware!

This book is already full of activities that require vulnerability as participants focus inward. Being online only adds to that sense of vulnerability. *It's not just me online. My family is in the same room with me; you want me to share out loud in front of them? You want me to do what moves in front of them? Are you crazy?*

Then, there's the added pressure of staring face-to-face with all the others in your group, and, at a camera. *A CAMERA!!!! Are you kidding me? I feel like my whole group is staring right at me. Are they judging me? Are they judging my room?*

Those comments aren't restricted to participants. Facilitators may feel such pressures too! This layer of vulnerability doesn't show up as obviously as when face-to-face where eyes stare at the ceiling, the floor, out the window, or at the head of the person in front of them.

The journey of this book is one of self-awareness, introspection, and action. The purpose is to help others become the best versions of themselves possible. Continue to be the guide and set the tone online. Be sensitive to how your whole group is essentially invading other people's personal space. Having a window into where people live can impact behaviors, attitudes, and dynamics.

Discuss with your group what you can do to keep the space safe and participants focused. Determine methods that will work for everyone to keep them engaged.

For example, in **Comfort Levels,** everyone responds using physical motions. You could ask your group to look down, turn their seats sideways to stare off to the side, put their backs to the screen to do the movements, OR chart/doodle on paper marks that represent their responses to each statement called out. By looking down, away, or to the back of the room, they have a needed screen break and encouragement to focus inward instead of on what others are doing. By doodling or charting, they have something to do with their hands while not looking at everyone else. The activity becomes a personal assessment.

Experiment. Try different methods. Together, find what works for your group so they can benefit the most from the activities provided while online.

Youth Specific Audience Ideas

I've already mentioned having people R.S.V.P. so that you know who's coming, enabling the waiting room, and locking the meeting. There are other things you should keep in mind when holding youth sessions. Many agencies have already established additional safety procedures to protect groups. Check with your agency to see what their policies are. Here are a few I've run across that seem fairly universal:

- **Monitor the group chat** to prevent bullying, sidebar conversations, or other ways that people can distract themselves on private chat.
- **Turn off screen sharing** permission for participants. You can always grant it later on an individual basis if it is needed and germane to what is going on in the meeting.
- **Follow any normal practices** of youth leading the meeting, taking attendance, keeping notes, etc. These routines help move your group forward in their leadership skills.
- **Consider a minimum of two approved adults** in place for the meeting or conference. Not only is it a good idea for co-hosting duties, it's also a sound practice of adult-to-youth ratios and support. As with in-person ratios, having more than one adult is important. These staff or volunteers should be first online before young people connect to welcome them when they come.
- **Look for new ways to involve youth leadership** by assigning roles as virtual facilitators. Let youth lead icebreakers or be facilitators in breakout sessions. They, too, can monitor access to the space, be time keepers, monitor questions in chat, etc.

 **Facilitator's Note**

A few more resources to keep your group safe and engaged. Ideas provided by 4-H:

Tips to Avoid Zoom "Bombers"—
https://ucanr.edu/sites/Professional_Development/
files/322864.pdf

Teaching Practices for Out-of-School Time Online
Learning Fact Sheet—
https://ucanr.edu/sites/UC4-H/files/325670.pdf

Integrating Experiential Education into Online
Learning Fact Sheet—
https://ucanr.edu/sites/UC4-H/files/325668.pdf

Online Still Means Paying Attention to Needs

Once you are comfortable with meeting online, you can turn your focus back to your group. How do I keep them interested, engaged, and contributing? How do I maintain the people-to-people connections that are so vital? How do I honor the different ways in which people learn best? How do I incorporate methods that help fuel brain development?

Below I've included some tried and true techniques you can try for yourself. Highlighted are a few brain boosters (movement, novelty, challenge), standard group developers (ice breakers, mixers, team games) and learning styles variations (art, kinesthetic, visual, interpersonal, intrapersonal).

Break the ice. Have an icebreaker question posted before the meeting starts. This way you can engage participants who show up early and/or kick off the meeting/training time informally—something they'd otherwise miss not being face-to-face.

Mix things up. A free resource online is the Wheel of Names. This spinner allows you to customize and input names, icebreaker questions, alphabet letters, and so forth onto the wheel. You spin it and voila! the random picker selects who goes next, what the next question is, etc. **Find here:** https://wheelofnames.com/

Incorporate movement. Since humans are not wired to sit for long periods of time, look for ways you can make what you teach more interactive. How can you incorporate movement? Drawing? Taking and posting photos? Remember the various ways in which people learn and apply that to the online world.

Include art. Art is a valuable tool to access a different part of the brain and allow creative expression. Where can you have participants draw individually or together? Art can also be created with words. One free resource that allows you to select colors, themes, and shapes to apply to words is the free Wordcloud generator. **Find here:** https://www.wordclouds.com/

Create a shared, collaborative space. Google Docs is a great place to share information where everyone can add in their ideas.

Using a shared creation also serves as a visual prompt that helps the visual learners in your group. Bonus! You can send everyone what they created for them to keep.

Add novelty. Our brains thrive on novelty and challenge. Use free virtual dice or spinners to determine how many people are to answer, what prompt they follow or reply to, etc. The randomness adds that bit of surprise and focus you might need. The technique mixes things up, keeps it up in the air, and adds engagement.

Find here:

- **Google dice roller**—easily accessible to most, only rolls 1 die at a time
- **Toy Theater** (https://toytheater.com/dice/)—select the dice type, select how many (up to 5), hit the throw button, has rolling sound effects
- **Wheel Decide** (https://wheeldecide.com)—free and has sound effects; you can embed it in an activity and also select the number of questions

Draw on their habitats as a resource. Virtual teaching means you now have as a resource the various settings where each of your participants are. How can you use that to your advantage? How can you incorporate in a non-invasive way their surroundings? Objects. Mementoes. Totems. Have the group go on a scavenger hunt to collect an item related to a topic you're talking about for show and tell.

Benefit from the chat feature. This gem lets everyone comment and ask questions. It allows you, as the facilitator, or your designated monitor to respond as needed either privately or to the whole group. The chat feature lets you share links that you want people to click on right away. And you can post instructions there for the activity you are currently doing or the topic you are pursuing so that latecomers can see what everyone is working on without you having to pause and catch them up. (You may have to post it a couple of times depending on how many others are chatting so that your information doesn't get lost.)

Don't forget that if some people join by phone, they may not be able to see questions that pop up in chat. Read aloud questions and then respond so that you include your audio-only participants.

More Ways to Engage Digitally

Beyond adding to your toolkit of methods, this section highlights a few techniques you can tap to lead some of the activities in this book online. Plus a few extra methods. Just because.

Thumb-o-meter—Here's an easy check-in technique to see how everyone feels about a given question. They hold their thumbs up if the answer is good, yes, etc. They wiggle their thumbs if they are iffy, unsure, so-so, etc. Finally, they hold their thumbs down if their answer is no, not good, etc.

Curiosity Tag—This icebreaker is a method that continues to build relationships and keep people actively engaged with one another. Kick it off by picking someone in the group. Ask them a question. Ask something you'd really like to know and are curious about. (For example, if you could spend the day with any mentor, who would you pick and why?). After they answer, have them "tag" the next person to go, and they get to ask a different question.

Icebreaker Scramble—Put 30 seconds on the clock and challenge your group to get up and find an object in their space that represents X (their personal brand, their leadership style, their personality, a goal that they are working to achieve, how they are feeling currently, an essential ingredient for making a team work effectively, and so forth). As you can see by the suggestions in the parentheses, this method is very versatile for exploring whatever topic you are leading. When everyone comes back, have members take turns explaining why they chose the object they did.

Vote with Your _____
For activities in which you want your group to choose between 2 or more options, you can have the group:
- Sit down for one option and stand up for the other.
- Lean one direction for the first option or lean the other for the second option. Left or right, toward the screen or away from it. Or, wiggle their fingers toward their screen or on either side of their head to indicate the two choices. Stand and slide to the left or right side of their screen—still staying in view.

- If using a white board or PowerPoint, you can draw a horizontal line down the middle of the board or slide to create 2 option choices or create 4 squares (for example, strongly agree/agree/disagree/strongly disagree) and have the group vote with their stamp (annotation feature on Zoom) by placing it in the indicated area that matches their answer.
- Use the chat feature. Invite everyone to record their answer in chat but hold off "casting" their vote until you give the signal. When ready, do a 3–2–1 countdown and have everyone cast their vote at the same time.
- Poll Everywhere and Slido have free online options you may want to use for polling answers.
  Find here: www.polleverywhere.com/ or at www.sli.do

Physical Indicators—You can have your group respond physically to posed questions using the whole body, mannequin positions, or their hands to indicate the verbal cues you give. For example, they can:
- Position their hands, right facing left, in front of their hearts to indicate "a little." They hold them a little wider than shoulders' length apart to indicate "some." They hold out their arms widespread to indicate "a lot."
- Scrunch their bodies in toward their stomach, stretch out their arms, or march in place to represent different comfort levels for taking risk.
- Fly their arms like Supergirl, put hands on hips and look off to the side, or point their finger in the air to represent respectively superhero strong, sidekick strong, or fan strong.

Buzz In—Just like it sounds, have participants rattle keys, hit the table, use a noise maker, buzz with their mouths, or use the thumbs up emoji to be the first person to chime in when they want to be the first one to answer a question.

Guess Who—You can have individuals use the chat feature to send the facilitator 3 facts about X (themselves, for example) that you read aloud and the others try to guess who the person is.

Rename Feature—Use this tool (located in your video square in the upper righthand corner) for 1-word check-in's as people enter the meeting or training or to answer an easy icebreaker question like "mountains or beach?" You can have participants identify their pronoun choices along with their name. You can also use the rename feature for participants to weigh in with their answer (like, "I choose answer 1, 2, 3, or 4") to a question. You can then divide people into breakout rooms based on their response. You may want to send them on a quick break while you look at their choices and divvy them into the breakout rooms.

To use the rename feature, have participants type in their name and their answer choice based on the format you set.

Breakout Rooms—Use these for any activity in which you want them to do small group work or pair-shares to discuss, create a skit, presentation, poem, etc. You can also use the rooms for individual timed work and for one-on-one conversations that might have been done as concentric circles if face-to-face. Or, you can use them for competitions such as—

Scavenger Hunts—Go over the directions in the big group. Put them in breakout rooms. Then broadcast what you need. The first group to type in private chat directly to the host or to come back with their object wins that round's point. (Note: Using the private chat feature ensures that only the facilitator sees the answers, not the other groups. Since the responses are time stamped, the host can scroll to see which group submitted a second before another group if the race is close.) If leading a scavenger hunt, you could also, after telling them directions and how much time they have, use the broadcast feature to send a message out simultaneously to all the breakout rooms to give them the list of items each of the teams needs to collect. When time is up, have everyone come back and see how each team did.

Team Challenges—The breakout rooms are also perfect for team building, competitions, and challenges. Giving directions while together in the big group, explain that each team will see 10, for example, team building challenges broadcast to their rooms, one at a time every 60 seconds. If you are purposeful about not stating that they only have 60 seconds to complete each challenge, then when you debrief the activity, you can focus more on the importance of playing to each other's strengths and experience and how individual contributions helped each team achieve their goals.

Be creative in the challenges you put out, for example, make a playlist of 10 songs that inspire them, name as many characters in the *Star Wars* movies as they can, collect one item per person on their team that starts with the first letter of each one's name, identify 10 foods everyone should try, find 8 GIFs for Disney movies they love, etc. You can also give them ahead of time words to unscramble and then name the one item that doesn't belong to the rest. They can take the shortest name in a given team and find things they have in common that start with each letter in the chosen name.

Chat Creations—Do group projects. Identify teams and have each team write down the order of who goes first, second, and so. Have the first person in each team jot down a line of a poem and send it to the second person and the facilitator. The second person silently reads the line and jots down a new line and sends only that line to the next person on their team plus the facilitator. After everyone has had a turn, ask each team to take turns reading their group poem aloud.

You can also have every participant finish a given sentence prompt such as "My best leadership trait is...." Chat prompts are great for icebreakers, feeling check-ins, and reflections on the session.

Tag Teams Method—Ask for 2 volunteers to start in whatever competition you are doing. If it's answering a question, for example, they might buzz in. If it's drawing something, they might draw and then hold the picture up for you to see. You run the competition, then those 2 people pick the next 2 people to compete thus building their team, one person at a time.

Lucky #s Throw Down (from Ann Saylor's and my book, *Great Group Games: Dice Edition*)—Have at least 2 people pair off to play a round of Rock, Paper, Scissors but in number style. They slap their fist into the palm of their other hand while they count 1, 2, and on 3, each person throws down anywhere between 1–5 fingers. As the facilitator you can choose the lower or higher number to determine an action with the number. For example, 5 people who will answer the question or 3 people who will participate in the next activity or 2 breakout rooms that will be created.

While the ideas included here are not exhaustive, it's a jumping off point for you to think about the space you create and how you can maximize the learning experience.

 Facilitator's Note

If you're a facilitator/leader and want to grow your techniques for group and personal development, reach out. Our books, coaching calls, or trainings might be just right for you. Happy to chat and see if we are a match for what help you need. You can contact us at team@WriteCreationsGroup.com or through our website at WriteCreationsGroup.com.

Bonus Materials

https://writecreationsgroup.com/bookbonuses

Behind the Scenes

Credits: Couldn't Have Done It Without Them!

Writing a book takes a village—editors, reviewers, designers, contributors, field testers, and people who listen to you, even when you go on and on about your book because you are excited or stuck. Many of those informal conversations sparked ideas, processes, or new directions for activities.

Nicole Givens Kurtz, you saved me. You helped me get out of a traditional box and framework and re-imagine leadership in a way that was more *me*. Combining sci-fi and fantasy genres gave me life and hopefully enlivened the book, as well. It made the writing all the richer.

Those of you who contributed activities or ideas, inspired wisdom or shared your experience, thank you! You sharpened my thinking and no doubt made this book more fertile because it reflects others in the field. That's always my goal. I love uplifting and honoring the work others are doing.

Here are particulars to give credit where it's due to those who introduced me to an activity, explained their unique take on it, then let me go at it in adapting it yet again:

Chapter 1

- What's My Style?—inspired by a conversation with Tina Corkum
- Forced Choices—used with permission by Carlos Morenzo, http://arizacarlosmoreno.blogspot.com
- Storytelling—Dr. Eli Parrot and Cherie Parker
- Red Carpet Conversations—Dr. Eli Parrot

Chapter 2

- In & Out—Jonna Laidlaw
- Self-ID—Laura Delgado
- Rolling Off the Tongue & Two By Four—from *Great Group Games Dice Edition: Crazy Challenges, Intriguing Icebreakers, Engaging Energizers*. Copyright ©2017 Susan Ragsdale & Ann Saylor, Nashville, TN. All rights reserved.
- Connect & Reflect & Define Your Vision—Dan Horgan

- Becoming Present: Be in the Story & Practicing Presence—Crys Zinkiewicz
- Meet-n-Greet—Spencer Bonnie
- Then, Now, Next—Ed Zinkiewicz
- Ultimate Team Member—Matt Gress

Nancy Dickson, you've held unswerving faith in me and have let me test SO many new ideas out with the Humphrey Fellowship Program at Vanderbilt University. To the team at STARS (Students Taking a Right Stand), thank you for participating and then testing activities, giving feedback, and being sounding boards along with valuable suggestions. To my awesome beta readers, advisors, and more street team testers: Chip Harris, Melanie Eby, Miranda J. Riley, Marci McClain, and Jonna Laidlaw. Every contribution you made, large or small, was incredibly insightful and made this book better. Thank you! Rebecca Kelley, you are the best! Merci! Dan Horgan, what a blast to partner together to lead the 10–Minute Toolkit live on Zoom chats where we spotlighted methods and activities. Another great tool to compliment this book. Check out the episodes on the Ragsdale & Saylor YouTube channel.

Crys Zinkiewicz, you are not only skilled as an editor, but you are also an awesome teacher. I am better because of you. Thanks for having such a great sense of humor and teaching me to cultivate the same about my own writing habits. Jeenee Lee, wow! The cover is SO beautiful. I just love it. Danielle Smith-Boldt, you turned words into something pleasing to scan and gave the insides so much umph in the layout. Linda Ragsdale, the icons you whipped out will make me happy for many books to come!

Final appreciation to Jim Nettles, of Author Essentials, Ann Saylor, partner in crime extraordinaire, and Pete Bobo, my number-one fan no matter what rabbit hole I go through. You all lead by example every day. And I am lucky enough to benefit from that.

About the Author

Susan Ragsdale is a nationally-recognized positive youth development specialist and a best-selling co-author with several titles to her name, including the best-selling *Great Group Games: 175 Boredom-Busting, Zero-Prep Team Builders for All Ages* and her latest, *Great Group Reflections: 60 Compelling Challenges to Prompt Self-Discovery & Critical Thinking.*

Through Write Creations Group, LLC, she influences how educators and youth workers engage with youth. She strongly believes **how you craft the experience matters.** Engaging others should be fun, experiential, relevant, and involve discovery. "Play, live, lead with purpose" is the both the mantra and the compass for all the work she does.

To that end, she and her partner in creativity, Ann Saylor, consult on training and curriculum development to add experiential activities to increase active participation. They also facilitate professional development workshops in leadership, team building, service-learning, training others, and youth development best practices. Often called "engaging" and "great presenters," their teaching is grounded in experiential learning, making workshops and curriculum fun while still maintaining depth and meaning.

Susan lives in Nashville with her husband Pete and their four-legged furball who graciously allows them to live there. If not writing, you can find her pursuing her wherever the creative muse takes her, which currently is working with mosaics and stained glass projects and putting out videos for Ragsdale & Saylor on YouTube.

Connect with Susan Online

Facebook @WriteCreationsGroup

Website: www.WriteCreationsGroup.com

Instagram: @WriteCreationsGroup

Twitter @Write_Creations

Want more tips, ideas, activities, and strategies?

Subscribe to Ragsdale & Saylor on YouTube at:
https://www.youtube.com/channel/UCuBiIot9a7CJQT_wq0S5-Hg

Sign up for the newsletter at:
www.WriteCreationsGroup.com

Like this book? Please write a review.
Reviews make a world of difference.

powerful publications • energetic trainings
write creations group

More Resources for You

I thought I would share some of the research and ideas that float around in my head and shape how I think. My natural bias is toward ideologies that inspire hope, focus on strength building, and help us become better versions of ourselves. I was blessed at any early age in my career to discover the work of Search Institute and their commitment to a strength-based approach when working with youth. I believe focusing on an at-promise approach rather than zeroing in on at-risk has greater rewards and cultivates a healthier mindset for everyone involved.

I hope you find these sources valuable to your work to develop people of promise. I know you'll find more tools!

- **Relationships First**—A free resource that gives a snapshot of what developmentally strong relationships look like. And, the *Relationship Check Tool*—*A tool for self-reflection and conversation among peers and within families.* Find both of these resources from Search Institute by going to https://www.search-institute.org/tools-resources/free-downloads/
- **Hardwired to Connect**—Learn more about the research tidbit referenced in a couple of the activities. Go to http://americanvalues.org/search/item.php?id=17
- **Growth Mindset**—Learn about fixed mindset versus growth mindsets, how to calculate, and even take an assessment at https://www.mindsetworks.com/science/
- **JoHari Window**—A communication tool that can reveal blind spots. Google this and you'll find models, videos, and images. https://www.communicationtheory.org/the-johari-window-model/
- **Storytelling Tools**—This site offers strategies to place storytelling at the center of social change and has a mix of free and buying options. Go here to learn more: https://www.storybasedstrategy.org/tools-and-resources
- **16personalities**—This site offers a free online assessment of natural tendencies and leadership styles. This could pair nicely with the What's My Style? Activity. The site also has some content on communicating and collaborating across styles that can feed into how personality tendencies impact leadership, communication, and team work. Find at https://www.16personalities.com/free-personality-test

Other Titles by Susan Ragsdale & Ann Saylor

from Write Creations Group, LLC

Great Group Reflections: 60 Compelling Challenges to Prompt
Self-Discovery & Critical Thinking
Great Group Games Dice Edition: Crazy Challenges, Intriguing
Icebreakers, Engaging Energizers

from Search Institute

Great Group Games: 175 Boredom-Busting Zero-Prep Team Builders
for All Ages
Great Group Games for Kids: 150 Meaningful Activities for
Any Setting
Building Character from the Start: 201 Activities to Foster Creativity,
Literacy, & Play
Great Group Games Cards on the Go: 50 Favorite Team Builders
Get Things Going! 85 Asset-building Activities for Workshops,
Presentations, and Meetings
Groups, Troops, Clubs & Classrooms: The Essential Handbook for
Working with Youth

from Free Spirit Publishing

Brain Boosters for Groups in a Jar®
Imagination Boosters for Groups in a Jar®

from Abingdon Press

Ready-to-Go Service Projects: 140 Ways for Youth Groups to Lend
a Hand

To Buy

To learn more or purchase any of these books, go to
https://writecreationsgroup.com/theshop/